Lasting Joys

Whenever people are making music together, at that time they are better human beings.

Yehudi Menuhin

Lasting Joys

Muriel Yendell

First published in 2005 by
Muriel Yendell
in co-operation with
The Salvation Army
UK Territory Literary Unit

ISBN: 0 85412 740 2

Printed and bound in Great Britain by
ProPrint
Riverside Cottages
Old Great North Road
Stibbington
Cambridgeshire
PE8 6LR

FOREWORD

I consider it a privilege to be asked to write a foreword to Muriel's memoirs. Mind you, even now when Muriel asks you to do something she says it in such a way that you simply cannot refuse!

I have known Muriel for most of my life. She transferred to Hendon Corps soon after the death of her first husband, and my brother and I were asked to look after her son, Andrew, in their early days at the corps. As a young person, my original impression of Muriel was of a very strong, formidable leader, totally in charge of any and every situation, and highly competent in whatever task she was undertaking.

Knowing that Muriel was a head teacher only enhanced the air of 'authority' she seemed to have. This perception of Muriel stayed with me for some years as I grew up in the corps. As a trainee teacher, my final teaching practice was at Northwood School, the school where Muriel was the head teacher. My respect for her only increased during that term at the school. She was an absolutely outstanding head teacher, and I can only say that, during the whole of my teaching career, she was amongst the best that I have worked with.

Subsequently I have worked with Muriel at numerous Salvation Army music schools and also in our years together as music leaders at Hendon Corps. As I have grown older, I have also grown to realise that there is far more to Muriel than revealed in the almost child-like perception I had of her when I was young! She has incredible enthusiasm and energy, courage, spiritual depth and, of course, talent! I have learnt so much from her about what it is to be a Salvation Army leader, and for that alone will always be in her debt.

But probably now, one of her greatest gifts is that of encourager. And her support and encouragement for me, and so many other leaders around the territory, is valued greatly.

In my opinion, Muriel Yendell has been one of the truly outstanding music leaders in the history of Salvation Army music making, and I am sure that her memoirs will make a fascinating read!

Stephen Cobb

Contents

CHAPTER ONE
'As it was in the beginning'.

'Excuse me; are you Mrs Yendell of the Salvation Army and Northwood School?' The speaker was seated at an adjacent table on the last evening of a Saga holiday in Ireland in the year 2000. My name had been called out as I had won a 'first-name-out-of-the-hat' competition.

'I know you, don't I?'

'Yes, I've been saying to my wife all week, "I'm sure that is Mrs Yendell".'

I dug deep into my memory; he was an adviser for the London Borough of Hillingdon, and Northwood School in that borough was where I spent the last fifteen years of my teaching career. I recalled that he was adviser for technical studies – a subject where I had needed quite a lot of advice! But his name eluded me. He then told me 'Mr Nicholson' and we spent the rest of the evening in pleasurable reminiscing. There I was, twenty years after my retirement, labelled 'Salvation Army' and 'Northwood School'! I had no trouble with the precedence given to the Salvation Army in his enquiry. I had been dedicated to God in the Salvation Army when I was a baby and I have been a Christian and a Salvationist all my life.

My father lived in Burnley, Lancashire, as a child and young man; his parents were the poorest of the poor, living in slum conditions. He and his older brother often had to keep the peace between their parents when they were very much the worse for drink. It had not been unusual for the boys to be without decent clothes, even after they had left school and started work in the weaving mills. Their suits were pawned to find money for alcohol. I remember as a young girl going on the tram to Burnley to see Granddad and Grandma Wilson. I would cling close to my father as we walked along the shabby street to the last house on the right. Always, without fail, there was a lady sitting at an open door: her face was terribly disfigured with cancer, and I shrank away as I passed by with eyes averted. Eventually Uncle Ben and

1

my father had no alternative but to leave home; it was the only way that they could be sure that their non-working clothes were available to them at the weekend. By contrast, my mother was brought up in a Christian home; her parents were members of the Salvation Army. The oldest of the family became a Salvation Army officer, despite the fact that she was little more than five feet tall. She was below the required height for officership but she must have impressed somebody in authority. 'They don't make diamonds as big as bricks,' was one of her favourite quotes; she was fondly known as 'The little Major' - Major Frances Roberts.

I am not aware how my parents met but they did tell me that my dad said to my mother, 'I won't stop you from going to 'the Army', but don't ask me to come with you'.

Mother must have been quite irresistible: she certainly looked lovely in her wedding photograph; both the bride and the groom were wearing Salvation Army uniforms. So much for 'Don't ask me to come with you'! Apparently Granddad Roberts refused to attend the wedding, his reason being that he was not prepared to 'give away' any of his daughters! That was a bit eccentric, a trait of which I saw no sign when I later used to play innumerable games of draughts with him.

Up to my seventh birthday, we lived at Brierfield. My father served as corps sergeant major and then as songster leader at the Salvation Army. In view of his upbringing and his minimal education – both my parents left school at the age of thirteen years – it was amazing that he soon became a good cornet player. Additionally, he had a beautiful singing voice and developed into an excellent tenor soloist. Some years later, after I had studied music and singing, he asked me to give him some help with his solo singing: I remember finding that very moving. As I write I can see the 'front room' where we did some work together at the piano.

'Dad, you are a lovely singer. All you need to do is some work on the words.'

During my career as a teacher, I have always encouraged and helped young people to discover the things that they can do well and persuade them to develop their talents. It is, of course, often a matter of chance whom you meet, which school you go to and what opportunities there are. I remember David, the son of Alf and Marjorie Ringham, who by chance went to a school where the physical education teacher was a fanatical basketball player and taught the game throughout the school. David discovered that he loved it and was an exceptionally talented player. On one occasion I accompanied the Ringham family to a basketball game where David was actually playing for England in the under-eighteen team. Had he attended a different school, he might never have known that at basketball he was good enough to play for England! At Northwood School, for example, he might have been a top class gymnast, as was one of the boys during my time there. The PE teacher was brilliant, specializing in gymnastics.

My parents' first baby died in infancy. Phillis Rose Wilson was my older sister and I was named Muriel after the wife of the doctor who delivered me. We both went to St. Paul's School, a Church School just inside the boundaries of Nelson; it is still functioning some seventy-plus years later. It was at school that I discovered that my sister was 'Phillis Rose', so I decided that I must be 'Muriel Rose' and accordingly put that name on all my school exercise books. When dad discovered this, he put a stop to it! Phillis and I walked to school together – she was five and I was three years old. We had a mile to walk – two little girls, one in front of the other. A lady, who lived in a cottage about three-quarters of the way, always looked out for us – both going to and from school. She usually gave us a biscuit. At that time, white lines were being painted down the middle of the roads. I asked dad,

'What are the white lines for?'

He replied,

'To remind drivers to keep to their side of the road.'

So, in my naïveté, I decided that walking to school on the white line was the safest thing to do – that seemed logical! When dad found out, he really made a big fuss and forbade me ever to walk down the middle of the road again.

During almost the whole of my school days, my parents were working as weavers in the cotton mills. Whilst we lived in Brierfield they had almost two miles to walk to work. The hours were 7.00 am to 5.20 pm, with thirty minutes for breakfast and an hour for lunch: no canteens – packed lunch! Weaving meant standing at the looms all day, often in damp conditions, particularly in the heat of summer when the cotton threads were dry and easily broken. During those times, steam would be pumped into the weaving shed making everything damp as it cooled; at least the weavers' feet were kept dry because their clogs, with irons on them, kept their feet well above the damp floor level. At home a minder would come in to supervise our breakfast and to see us off to school. When we came home from school in the afternoon we had to report to Mrs Waterland; she lived with her husband and four boys in the same row of houses as we did. School holidays were mostly spent under her supervision.

It seems I had a propensity for getting into trouble. On one very rainy day, when a down-pipe in the school playground was severely overflowing, someone pushed me under the 'waterfall' with the inevitable result – wet through. I chased and caught the perpetrator of the crime and held him under the deluge, after which he ran into school crying and very wet. Soon too, I was ordered into school, very much in trouble. When they noticed my wet dress, they questioned the boy who admitted he had started it! He was not the innocent victim he had pretended to be! Of course my sister told my dad what had happened and then I was in more trouble. My first visit to hospital followed another of my escapades. At the back of our row of houses, each occupier owned a fenced strip of land. My dad kept hens and grew vegetables; the Waterlands had a hut in their 'hen pen'. One day Phillis and I were playing with two of the boys, chasing each other round the hut. At one point one of the boys changed

4

direction and accidentally charged right into me. My arm was hurt and I cried; so they put me in the hut 'until you stop crying'. But I didn't stop. My dad was working in his garden some fifty yards away and I heard his voice calling,

'Where's our Muriel?'

'She's in the shed.'

'Why?'

'She's hurt her arm.'

'Bring her to me,'

Dad immediately took me to the hospital in Nelson, a mile and a half downhill walk! As a family we never had our own transport. A broken arm (greenstick fracture) was diagnosed; no plaster was needed but a sling securely fastened my arm to my body and was not to be removed for six weeks. We walked the one and a half miles back home up the hill; the six weeks of discomfort and handicap seemed to last for a very long time!

Shortage of money was a real problem for my parents. The General Strike of 1926 hit the cotton industry hard and my parents had neither work nor income. Our next-door neighbour regularly received parcels of provisions from her daughter who lived on a farm; this generous lady would give some to my mother, saying,

'She's sent more than I can use. Would you like some?'

To my parents it was literally a Godsend. My dad and a fellow-Salvationist hitch-hiked into the Cumbrian countryside taking with them their cornets – the only way they could earn some money, most of which was sent home. When dad came back home there were lots of interesting stories to hear of people's kindness and concern, of being asked to play at celebrity events and especially of an invitation to play at a party in the grounds of a village Manor House, where not only were they well paid but were also well fed!

At some point I was considered old enough to have spending money, and was given a halfpenny a week, which later rose to one penny and much later to two pence - I had to be a good girl to earn a rise. I was very careful not to spend my money all at once. There was a terrible episode when I did a dreadful thing; I remember it in every detail. My dad gave me two pennies to pay for the Salvation Army papers – *The War Cry* and *The Young Soldier*. Instead of doing that, I spent it on sweets at the little shop down the road. Stupidly I had failed to realise that my sins would find me out; as soon as the lady in charge of distribution of the papers asked my dad for the money, nemesis was sure to follow. It did and I was taught a lesson the hard way – no more pocket money for the time being and I was made to feel really ashamed of myself. There was no corporal punishment: just expressions of disappointment and an atmosphere of sadness – far more potent than the cane! The sense of shame overcame me on the next Sunday during the evening meeting at Brierfield Salvation Army. The captain was walking up and down the aisles during the prayer meeting, inviting people to the 'mercy seat'. Seated at the end of the form (no chairs!) I reached out, caught her arm and asked if I could 'go out to the front'. She went with me and prayed with me. I could only have been six years old, but it left me with a real experience of forgiving love. One should never underestimate the power of the Holy Spirit to work in the lives of even the youngest children:

> *'If with all your hearts ye truly seek Me, ye shall ever surely find Me'.* (Deuteronomy 4:29)

Music was not a big item in my early life, but I do remember my dad playing his cornet whilst marching round the front room (not parlour . . . not sitting room . . . not lounge in those days) with Phillis and me marching behind him. My only other musical experience was an abortive attempt to join the singing company. When I became seven years old I started going to practices and was kitted out with uniform. It is the hat that I remember! Plain natural-colour straw hats were quite cheap; one was bought for me and then dyed a deep navy blue. With the regulation Salvation Army band around it, my uniform was complete. So the date was set for my enrolment – my sister was already in the singing company. However, the leaders discovered that the appointed date was somewhat premature, I would have to wait several months until my eighth birthday. To me that seemed grossly unfair. Someone had made a mistake and I was being punished. So there and then I decided that I wanted nothing more to do with the singing company. It was an incident that affected my attitude in later years when I myself was in the teaching situation. 'It isn't fair', is usually a cry of anguish. Children and young people will forgive most things – but not unfairness. As a teacher, one of my tenets was 'firm, fair and fun'. One day, many years later, I remember a boy at school, who came bursting into my room. He was in quite a state and said to me without preamble:

> 'It isn't fair! He's sent me to you to be caned because I swore at him. But he swore at me first – you won't punish him, will you? I'm the one that's going to be punished.'

Quite an outburst in the head teacher's room! It was one of those occasions when I felt some sympathy for the miscreant, whilst at the same time knowing that I had to avoid creating more problems by revealing to him my displeasure with the member of staff: the accusation of swearing was totally credible. So I dealt with the boy: swearing at members of staff was not acceptable. Later I dealt with the teacher: swearing at pupils was equally unacceptable – totally unprofessional.

Soon after the singing company episode, we all moved to Nelson to live with my mother's parents; they were considered to be 'getting old' - Grandma was fifty-five years and Granddad sixty-five years old! That was in 1928. It was quite an upheaval for Phillis and me: we moved to Whitefield School. On the site was an infants' school for five to seven year-olds. By age I should have joined the infants' school but a letter from St. Paul's, presented to the head teacher, caused me to be taken to the 'big' school, which my sister had already joined. I was pleased about that, but not so happy when I soon had my knuckles rapped for making blotches when underlining words in my exercise book. I was using pen and real ink of the liquid variety, which I had never previously used. Again, I felt that my punishment was unfair. Later I suffered a further assault on my pride. Apparently, (unlike my sister) I was not very good at needlework. One terrible day the teacher sent me, with sub-standard needlework, to my sister's class; my needlework had to be compared to hers in full view of the whole class. I was humiliated. It was another situation that had a profound effect on me and on my future dealings with young people.

Probably my worst episode was an act of gross unfairness and vindictiveness – the worst I have ever suffered. I was in the 'scholarship class' and was aware that the teacher, a Miss L, was not over-fond of me: a girl named Winifred was justly known as the 'teacher's pet'! During an arithmetic lesson, we were doing lots of sums and had to line up at the teacher's desk to be marked every four sums. I was getting along fine – all the sums correct, lots of ticks! But, whilst standing in the queue, I dared to speak to the person next to me. A stentorian voice boomed out:

'Muriel Wilson, did you speak?'

'Yes, Miss.'

'Bring your book here.'

She marked it – all correct. Then she threw my book into a back corner of the room.

'Follow your book and stay there until I tell you to move.'

I was mortified! Out of the corner of my eye I could see my rival going to and from the teacher's desk until the teacher spoke to the whole class:

'Winifred is the first to finish. She got all her sums right. Now Muriel Wilson, you may come out of the corner.'

After all these years, I can see the classroom, the people in it and the teacher concerned. I can remember vividly my feelings of humiliation, unfairness and considerable anger. Is it any wonder that as a teacher I always tried to be fair and as a head teacher, I preached this gospel to my members of staff?

However, it was at Whitefield School that I first began to appreciate music and enjoy singing in a good choir. Mrs Hurst, the music teacher, awakened in me whatever musicianship I possessed and from that time onwards music became an important part of my life. I loved being in the school choir and getting involved in its activities. In addition to the lunchtime choir rehearsals, we all went back to school on Friday evenings for an intensive rehearsal. The same music teacher also gave private lessons at one shilling and sixpence per session – both piano and singing. My parents found the money to pay for Phillis to have a weekly piano lesson. Their combined wages would have been about three pounds a week: during the 'hard times' my mother sent a weekly two shillings and sixpence postal order to my Auntie Frances, who was stationed as a Salvation Army Officer in the depressed areas of Wales. Looking back, I have no recollection that Phillis and I ever felt a sense of deprivation. All our needs were met and we were loved!

Phillis became an excellent pianist and a top-class accompanist. She was later the pianist for Nelson Songsters and did the accompaniments at several music schools, including the national singing company camps. Her playing can be heard on some recordings of the London Girl Singers and she often played the pianoforte accompaniments for Maisie Ringham's trombone solos. She continued to live in Nelson and was a well-known piano teacher, as well as being the official accompanist for local music festivals. One day my dad found me playing the piano: *Smallwood's Piano Tutor* had some easy pieces on the first pages and I worked it out for myself. He asked me whether I would like to have lessons.

I replied, 'Yes please.'

'I'll talk to your mother and see what we can do.'

The upshot was that I began to have piano lessons with Mrs Hurst. After about two years I persuaded my dad that I was not going to be a good pianist – not a patch on Phillis. So I gave up piano lessons, and as a result, my sister was able to have singing lessons as well. That was when Phillis and I started playing piano duets – much less solitary than practising alone: this kept my piano playing going and no doubt improved my sight-reading and actual piano work. It was not until some years later that I had piano tuition again.

Both my sister and I enjoyed our time in the Whitefield School choir – it was wonderful. We took part in competitive music festivals throughout Lancashire and Yorkshire, always obtaining high marks and generally taking first prize. Our archrivals, a girls' school from Blackpool, forced us into second place on one, and only one occasion. Obviously our music teacher was an exceptionally gifted choral trainer: The Lancashire and Yorkshire festivals were renowned for their high standard. I believe that I absorbed much of what is best in choral music in those formative years.

At some point my father bought me a mandolin at a local auction; it cost a fortune – two shillings and sixpence!

'See if you can play it Muriel' he said.

Once I knew how to tune it up (the same as a violin) it was fine. Much later he had the opportunity to buy a banjolin: it had the appearance of a banjo but was strung like a violin. It was a most unusual instrument, something of a rarity but it made a lovely sound. When my sister acquired a piano accordion we began to play together. Music was very important in our household; dad was still playing cornet and singing, Phillis and I practised piano duets and sometimes the three of us would be making music together.

When having won a 'scholarship', I moved to what was called Nelson Secondary School, which was the equivalent of today's grammar schools, the only music available was class singing. Music-wise, my five years there were almost a waste of time. I did, however take part in a school concert, singing a duet with 'Georgie' in a question and answer ditty, *There's a hole in my bucket*. I remember clearly my acute embarrassment when I was taken into a full staff room to try on a 'milkmaid-type' costume. Taking off my gymslip and blouse revealed my multi-patched vest: the family could not buy vests as well as the many compulsory items of school uniform.

My ambition had always been to become a teacher: it seemed to be an interesting and worthwhile way to earn a living. This would have involved two years at a training college which would be financially impossible. After one year in the sixth form, I decided to leave school and managed to get work in a mill office, and then told my parents. My sister had left school when she was fourteen and worked as an apprentice to a master baker. When I, too, started to earn ten shillings a week which rose to thirty shillings after two years, my mother was able to quit working at the mill. Phillis and I had to hand over our wages to dad, from which he gave us what he considered an appropriate amount of spending money. As I was working in an office I decided to go to evening classes to follow a commerce course which included English, commerce, book-keeping, typewriting and shorthand. I had already taken and passed the 'subsidiary' levels examinations – the equivalent of today's O/A levels. The commerce course was enjoyable and the qualifications would be useful. My work in the mill office was not difficult once I had learnt to use the Burrough's adding machine, which was a clumsy forerunner of today's calculators: nor was it by any means time-consuming. I found myself with many periods of time with nothing to do; the proverbial devil found work for my idle hands.

The manager of the weaving mill had a small office in the warehouse. It was really just a corner, which formed two of his office walls, and two added walls completed his 'space'. The larger of the two sides had a window and a door. When the manager, Joe, was needed by my boss, the office girl had to go in search of him – no mobile phones or phone extensions! The first place to look was his office: if his keys were in the door, he was inside. Previously I had warned him that one day someone would lock his door and take the key away, then what would he do? On one of our quiet days I decided to prove my point and took the

11

keys out of the door, adding insult to injury by dangling them at him from outside his window. My intention was to release him after five minutes' captivity. However some work came onto my desk so I got on with it. It was not until the next morning that I remembered: Joe had not been released! What had happened to him? Had he been in captivity all night? Was he still alive? How could I go to work and face the music? I still shudder at the thought of it. However, there was no alternative, because telling my dad what had happened would bring retribution far worse than what might happen at work. So, with trepidation, I caught the usual tram that would take me to my fate. Of course Joe was FURIOUS!!! He had been forced to take off the door lock when someone had gone to see him: he felt that he had been made to look stupid. I was mortified and apologetic. Until then our relationship had been good; it took a long time for that relationship to be restored. A valuable lesson had been learnt.

Not being prepared to do boring office work all my life I looked towards the civil service and decided to try for the clerical grade. To prepare for the examinations I undertook a correspondence course. However, a chance encounter at evening school with the principal, a Mr Duerden, who had taught me chemistry at my day school, changed the whole direction of my life. Was this meeting really chance? Or was God already working in my life to guide me into the path that I was to follow? Mr Duerden asked me:

'How are you getting on? What are you doing? Do you like your job?'

My negative reply to the last question brought another question:

'What are you going to do about it?'

I told him about my ambition to be a teacher, but explained that finance was a problem, and in any case there was no point in applying because I had no 'A' levels. He persuaded me that it would be worth my while to apply to a college and suggested that, as I was keen on music, Sheffield Training College, which had a good reputation for music, would be an excellent choice. At that point in time I had not a single music qualification – not even an 'O' level. When I returned home and told my parents about the conversation, the matter was discussed at some length. I myself was pinning my hopes on the civil service. The following day, my father said to me:

'Your mother and I have been talking'.

He told me that, in order for me to be able to go to college, my mother was prepared to go back to the drudgery of the mill. What a sacrifice! She was prepared to commit herself to two years of unremitting toil. I felt then, and still feel now, that she could never be adequately repaid. I did what I could and made every effort later on in my career to ensure that she was with me for the big occasions – speech days at school, school concerts and such special events as when the National Songsters sang at St. Martins-in-the-Field in Trafalgar Square in the presence of HM Queen Elizabeth, the Queen Mother. She was also present at the Royal Albert Hall in 1963, when I had the privilege of conducting the massed songsters at the council's festival. I did actually sit the Civil Service Examination and was offered a place in London – that was in 1939. However, my application for Sheffield City Training College was being processed and I had been called for an interview. So, taking a risk, I turned down the civil service offer. But all was well – I was accepted at Sheffield and excitedly prepared to go to college in September 1939.

At the age of seventeen years I had become a songster at Nelson – my dad was the songster leader – so not only was it the natural thing to do, it was also the wisest. My sister was the pianist and we were already involved in making instrumental music together, which we both enjoyed. I was eighteen years old and I was going to college to train as a teacher; my cherished ambition was about to be realised! The war started in September 1939 so the beginning of term was delayed until November because of the necessary building of air-raid shelters. Having already left the mill office, I needed some form of income and applied for a temporary job, which was the preparation of ration books for the whole of Nelson. It was a matter of great urgency to get these books out to the public and we must have worked hard, as the job was finished in two weeks. So I soon found myself jobless again. *Nil desperandum!* Of temporary jobs there were quite a number. I applied for and obtained work in the 'fuel office', preparing the details of and issuing coal/coke ration books. At my interview I had to spell 'anthracite' and also take a typing test – my commercial course came in very useful. I was still in that office when in November, a letter arrived to say that the college term was starting.

From then on the holidays were shortened in an effort to catch up with the course work. Things were made worse when, in December 1940, Sheffield was bombed and the college was damaged. One of the male students on fire-watch duty was killed and another injured. We spent two nights in the air-raid shelter, which had been in fairly frequent use the whole time I was at college and were left to get home as best we could. Four of us heading in the same direction were fortunate enough to get a taxi, which took us to the home of one of our number, whence a telephone call to a friend in Nelson brought a car to pick me up. It was a huge relief to get home. The first time I heard the new 'whistling' kettle I practically jumped out of my skin! Repair work at the college took a long time and it was the end of January before we could get back to Sheffield. On account of this and the delayed start of the first term, as well as nights spent in the air-raid shelters, all holidays had to be curtailed and the two-year course was crammed into eighteen months.

Teaching practice was a most interesting part of the course: every school we went to was unique, and I found it all very exciting. It was while I was teaching in a junior school in Sheffield that I learned that there can be more than one correct answer to a question. The use of paragraphs had to be taught to my class of 9–10 year olds in an 'oral composition lesson'. We chose a popular subject and the children started to suggest what could be written on the blackboard. Questions from me elicited the subject matter; I carefully wrote the children's sentences on the board and indented a line every now and then to produce paragraphs. After the last sentence and the final full stop, I asked the question:

> 'Do you notice anything special about what I have written on the blackboard?'

Lots of hands shot up: then a few more, until only one boy – Alec still had not responded. A chorus of 'Miss, Miss!' was coming from the more vociferous members of the class, along with much eager hand waving. Patiently I waited, reasoning to myself that even Alec, who was admittedly somewhat backward, could see that the lines did not all start at the same place. I would be satisfied with a comment about that. Finally and slowly Alec, with a knowing smile on his face, raised his hand.

> 'Ah! Alec. You've seen something. What have you noticed about the writing on the board?'

> 'It isn't very good writing Miss.'

> 'Well done, Alec. Good answer. Now has anyone noticed anything else?' Almost immediately I had the second and sought-for answer:

> 'You have started some of the lines a bit in from the side.'

Both the pupils and the teacher were a little wiser at the end of that lesson!

I had opted to take music as a special subject and joined the college choir, which amalgamated with the Sheffield City Choral Society for their oratorio performances – our music tutor was the Sheffield choir's chorus master. It was at that time that I first became acquainted with Mendelssohn's *Elijah*. Many years later it was my joy to use excerpts from *Elijah* with the Hendon Songster Brigade. On my first Sunday at college, I wore my Salvation Army uniform and I have to admit that it was not an easy thing to do. However, the only reaction was one of curiosity. Thereafter each Sunday I went to the Sheffield Citadel Corps, which was swarming with Air Force personnel! I sang with the songsters but was not able to attend rehearsals – our 'exit' times from college were limited and strictly controlled.

At the appropriate time I applied to Nelson Education Authority for a teaching post in a senior school. During all my teaching practice at college, I had taught in primary schools, but my preference was for older pupils and for the opportunity to specialise in music. When I was informed of my appointment, I could have been knocked down by the proverbial feather! It was to Whitefield School where I had been a pupil for over three years. The school was not far from where I lived so that was most convenient. But I would have walked miles to any other school; the head teacher, who had to be contacted, was none other than my all-time least favourite teacher – Miss L of the book- throwing incident! Ever the optimist, I hoped for the best but feared the worst.

* * *

CHAPTER TWO
'The best way to escape from a problem is to solve it'.
(Brendon Francis)

Thus in 1941 I went back to Nelson a qualified but probationary teacher. At the Salvation Army I was nominally a songster and my dad expected me to take up where I had left off. At Sheffield Citadel, I had not been in a position to be a one hundred per-cent member of the songster brigade – unable to get to rehearsals, not available for Saturday events and not involved socially. My father, however, took it for granted that on returning home I would immediately take up my place in the songster brigade. He was the songster leader, and I could not find it in my heart to disappoint him: both he and my mother had made tremendous sacrifices for me. Sadly, my father died two years later at the age of fifty-two. We were distraught.

The songster sergeant had once been the songster leader, so she took on the responsibility for the brigade for the time being. This state of affairs lasted until April 1945 when I was commissioned songster leader. It had taken a long time for the decision to be made, as the Deputy Songster Leader Rennie Richardson was serving in HM Forces in North Africa, and the entrenched local officers at Nelson did not want a young, modern, female songster leader, especially as she played tennis, badminton and netball. However, when Rennie had been contacted for his opinion on the matter, he advised the Commanding Officer Major Sydney Evans to appoint me. I was keen to do it because when I had tried to persuade my dad to relinquish the position, his answer was invariably,

'Nay! I'll keep going until Rennie gets home.'

My father had a serious heart condition. A Salvation Army bandsman – the only cornet player, due to most of the band being in the HM Forces – he was also the songster leader of a brigade with lots of female singers, but only two men – except for when those in the Forces came home on leave. Additionally he had become a town councillor with all the extra work thereby entailed. As was our custom, on Christmas Eve 1943, we had visited Uncle Ben and family in Brierfield. We then had an uphill walk to visit the Pollard family. At midnight, the whole party would go out-of-doors and sing – in four part harmony - *Hail Smiling Morn.* That year my dad excused himself – he could not face the uphill walk. No cars! No buses! So he went home alone.

'Enjoy yourselves! Stay as long as you like,' he urged us.

Soon after midnight I went to the nearest telephone box, and rang him to see if he had arrived home safely.

'Don't worry! I'm all right.'

The next morning, he went out Christmas playing with the band. He was the only cornet player, and by the last carol he was too exhausted to play. So, accompanied by the band, he sang it in his beautiful tenor voice.

'I'll keep going until Rennie gets home,' he had said.

Well, he kept going until Christmas day 1943, then collapsed and died that evening. I have always admired that example of dedication and perseverance.

By that time I had been teaching for two years, and my worst fears had been realized - the head teacher had not changed from the class teacher I had as a schoolgirl. In those days we were expected to teach any and almost every subject. During my stay at Whitefield School I was required (at some time or other) to teach English, mathematics, science, physical education (boys and girls), needlework and music with the boys. I soon recognized the sadistic tendencies of my 'boss' when we had the problem with the piano.

For a newly-qualified teacher of twenty years of age, teaching music to a class of fourteen-year-old boys was no picnic. The school had no equipment for listening to music: there were very few, and not very suitable songbooks and a piano that doubled as the piano for school assemblies. It was kept in the school hall, right next to the head teacher's desk and adjacent to my classroom. Resting on two centrally placed wheels, and with four wooden wedges to fix it in position as needed, it had to be wheeled in and out of my classroom. However, that was not too difficult once I had secured some willing help from the nearest hefty boys. It was great fun, especially under the eagle eye of the head teacher.

One day, however, when I was starting the manoeuvre to get the piano into the classroom, her stentorian voice boomed at me,

'Miss Wilson, you use the piano too much. From now on, you will have one week with, and one week without the piano. This will be the week without.'

I was astounded! Speechless! We went into reverse, and wheeled the piano back to its place near the head teacher's desk. At that time, and in my first year of teaching, I was not aware that she had no power to make and enforce such a decree: it seemed to have the authority of a royal command! Some good did come out of it, though. The boys had seen this: I explained the position to them, and said I would find some songs we could sing unaccompanied and try to get a 'gramophone' so that we could listen to music. They were clearly on my side!

There were times during the 'no piano' week when she was not at her desk. I would therefore try to sneak the piano into the classroom, being determined not to be totally subjugated. But all that stopped when one day, as I pushed the piano into my classroom, that dreaded voice was heard:

'Miss Wilson, is this the week with or the week without piano?'

Meekly, and resignedly going into reverse, I quietly said,

'The week without.'

When the female PE teacher moved away, I then had to take on that responsibility. My training for teaching PE was minimal: I would benefit from some expert tuition. Not qualified to use apparatus, I applied to go on a course during the school holidays at Loughborough College. It was tough going but proved to be just what I needed: now I had the qualification to at least use portable apparatus. There was no gymnasium at Whitefield School; all PE lessons were in the central hall – again under the eagle eye of the head teacher. Nevertheless this time she did not interfere. I think she knew that the PE master would soon be 'called up', and that she would need me to do his job. I enjoyed teaching PE, and it kept me fit: not that I relished the wintry days when I supervised the boys playing soccer in the nearby park.

In Nelson, the authority took much pride in the fact that all pupils were taught to swim whilst still at school. The town produced both an Olympic champion – Mary Kenyon, and a National Champion Boys' Relay team. I was not surprised that whatever the weather, I had to escort groups of pupils to and from the local swimming baths, a walk of about one mile each way. It was always something of a nightmare! Getting the children to the baths on time was easy – they were all keen to get there. Getting them back to school in time was the problem: they were the proverbial snails! If we were due back at school at, for example, 10.30 am, and we arrived at 10.33 am, that voice which I knew so well would bellow at me:

'Miss Wilson, you are three minutes late.'

There was little respite. On one occasion dressed in my PE kit, I ran through the central hall – obviously I was in a hurry.

'Miss Wilson , you should not be running in the school hall.'

In those days I was always an 'early bird'. I sometimes jocularly say that I have wasted years of my life being early! It was normal for me to arrive at school at 8 am, to make sure that everything was prepared for my classes, and that all my records and marking were up-to-date. At the end of the afternoon school I would be ready to leave at about 4.20 pm. But she would be sure to catch me.

'Miss Wilson, you should not be leaving school so early. Surely you have some marking to do.'

Then there came a turning point. She decreed that in each arithmetic lesson of one hour, I was to do mental arithmetic for at least half the time. That was a long 30 minutes! I had found it better to do a short, sharp spell of mental arithmetic, then some written work – sums that had to be marked – then some more mental arithmetic in preparation for the second set of written work. It was going well – until the day when the head teacher came into the classroom to find the whole class doing written work; clearly they had not had their thirty minutes' worth of 'mental arithmetic'. Without a word to me, she said,

'All put your pens down, and sit up straight – arms folded.'

I went and sat at my desk where I stayed, stony-faced, for the next twenty minutes, during which she gave me a demonstration lesson on how it should be done! She then stopped the lesson, turned to me, and said,

'Now, Miss Wilson!'

I stayed put! I intended to stay at my desk until she was outside the closed door. It was a battle of wills. When eventually she stalked out, I quietly said to the motionless, silent pupils,

'Now pick up your pens, and carry on where you were when the lesson was interrupted.'

It became clear to me that this head teacher was behaving in an unprofessional way, and that the only thing I could do was to stand my ground and not be intimidated. That was a lesson well learned; it helped me during the whole of my teaching career, and I'm sure, made that head teacher pause for thought. It was at that point I made a decision: as soon as I felt confident enough to believe that I could manage successfully whatever teaching situation came my way, I would apply to the local authority for a transfer to another school.

My class control, and therefore my teaching, was improving all the time, and so was my confidence. A kindly deputy head – a Mr Watson – was a tower of strength. He helped me, he advised me, and congratulated me when I managed to cope with a difficult situation. I decided to establish my right to have the piano in my classroom – and I got away with it. Finding a short musical play about pirates, I started to teach it to the older boys. They loved it! I said we would put it on for the whole school at the Christmas concert. But the head teacher had not finished with me yet! She came into my room whilst we were learning one of the songs,

'What is that song you are teaching them?'

'It is from a musical play.'

'What is it about?'

'Pirates.'

'Is it on your syllabus?'

'No, it isn't.'

'Then you cannot teach it in lesson time!'

It was useless to argue. She stalked out. The boys had heard it all.

'Never mind, we'll do it!'

So that is what we did. I promised them we would have it ready for the Christmas concert. I believe they worked for my sake as much as for their own pleasure. The musical was a huge success. From then on the head teacher more or less left me alone to get on with my job but I was still determined to move when I could get a transfer to another school. Although at that time there was much unpleasantness for me in that situation, I later realized that I had been taught some important lessons, much of which was of tremendous help to me when I moved into teaching posts that carried some extra responsibilities. Teaching is not an easy job and young inexperienced teachers need support, advice and encouragement from senior staff.

It was at the end of my time at Whitefield School, that I embarked on my career as songster leader, and discovered that choral training was not the only thing I had to learn – I had to learn to manage in an adult situation. My first problem is a good example. There were about twenty-four ladies in the group, and just two men who were too old to be in HM Forces: the bandmaster (tenor) and the deputy-bandmaster (bass). Both had very good voices. I had noticed that the bandmaster did not attend songster practices but I didn't know why. So on becoming the leader, I asked him. His view was that as he was the bandmaster and could read music, there was no reason for him to come to songster practice and to expect him to do so was somewhat insulting. I pointed out the need to be familiar with the words and also with the leader's interpretation: to no avail. Obviously there was only one acceptable outcome – so the bandmaster had to make a decision. This he did, and from that point on we had no tenors – i.e. until the men started to return to 'Civvy Street'. As there were some good singers and music readers amongst the ladies, I was able to use a few on the tenor part when it was essential e.g. *Glory, Glory!* [words: G.K. Johnson, music arranged by E. Leidzén] which has a tenor counter-melody. Many years later I found myself directing the National Songsters and using the same method when we wanted to sing a four-part song. From SATB (soprano, alto, tenor and bass) we successfully changed to SSAA, e.g. *The Road of the Pilgrim* [words: A. Wiggins, music: Don Osgood].

Another problem was the rather straight-laced lady, who, not wanting this youngster as songster leader, decided not to look at the conductor during both rehearsals and performances. I remember that she sat to the left of my music stand, so she effectively looked straight past me. I tried everything. I pointed out the need and that it was a matter of watching the conductor, not me personally,

'But we do watch you, Muriel,' was the exasperated cry from some other singers. Nothing would avail. So, reluctantly, I moved my stand directly in front of the lady – now she could see me even if she wasn't co-operatively looking. I must say, she soon graciously abandoned her protest, and my music stand went back to its normal central position.

The war ended and the songster brigade grew: now we had some tenors! The deputy songster leader came home, and I immediately offered to 'stand down' so that he could take over my job – thus keeping my pledge to fulfil my father's wishes. Rennie Richardson did not accept my offer. In the days when female songster leaders were a rare breed (I think I was one of only five in the territory at that time) this man put his faith in me, and graciously continued as deputy songster leader. He was a tower of strength. So was the saintly Songster Sergeant (Maggie Taylor) who, when I wanted to rush into dealing with a problem, would invariably tap me on the shoulder, and say,

'I would sleep on it if I were you, Muriel.'

So like many Salvationists, I took on a task that was challenging, somewhat daunting, and yet a wonderful opportunity for service in a unique way. I had become responsible for the choral work of a group of Salvationists whose service was meant to make a positive contribution to the spirituality of the corps. I believed then, and still do today, that this is the *raison d'être* of the songster brigade.

* * *

CHAPTER THREE

*'Do your best to present yourself to God as one approved and a
workman who does not need to be ashamed'.*
(2 Timothy 2:15)

Three years at Whitefield School were more than enough; I asked
the education authority for a transfer to another senior school. By
that time I could manage anything that the Whitefield head
teacher could throw at me. What I didn't have (to my shame), was
the guts to tell her that I was trying to get a move. I knew there
would be big trouble when it happened, and as a move was
dependant on a vacancy occurring elsewhere, I decided to 'wait
and see'. She was furious when the offer of a transfer came
through and 'sent me to Coventry', refusing to give me either a
reference or testimonial. Two years earlier she would probably
have been glad to get rid of me!

I could hardly believe the difference between the two schools
– the atmosphere at my new school, Bradley, was benign. The
head teacher, a Mr Crabtree, was a scholarly yet avuncular figure.
He was a wonderful raconteur and would hold both pupils and
staff in rapt attention as he spoke to the whole school at morning
assembly. He shared the staff room with us at break times, where
he often regaled us with fascinating stories of his experiences. He
didn't notice the time, and those of us who did, paid no attention
to it; the children were outside enjoying a break, one poor
member of staff was out with them, and we others were enjoying
ourselves. Then Mr Crabtree would take his watch out of his
waistcoat pocket, and a look of surprise would sweep across his
face. He would then say,

'Perhaps we'd better get them back in!'

The war ended in 1945 and the men and women in the Forces
started to return to 'Civvy Street'. Celebrations of VE Day were
ecstatic. My sister and I were taken to Burnley by Herbert Morris,
the bandmaster of Burnley Citadel. We sat atop the back seat of
his convertible car, Phillis playing her piano accordion and
everybody else, both in and out of the car, singing at the tops of

their voices. Flags were flying, streamers were streaming and everybody was cheering. Unforgettable!

As the men returned to the songsters, the bass section increased from one to six, and the tenor section from nil to three. Then we acquired a first rate tenor – Don Johnson – who had got himself engaged to one of my friends in the songster brigade. Soon we had a mixed choir of twenty-five ladies and eleven men – quite a good balance. Most Salvation Army songster brigades have a numerical imbalance of males and females, but experience has taught me that men join a songster brigade because they have good voices and enjoy singing: this generally compensates for lack of numbers.

Now that the bandmaster-who-didn't-need-to-come-to-songster-practices had resigned, and the lady-who-preferred-not-to-watch the songster leader had capitulated, I thought it would all be plain sailing. Had I been more experienced in directing a choir, I would have known better. I was about to learn that democracy in a songster brigade is a snare and a delusion. We were due to go to a nearby corps to present a Saturday evening programme. As all the men were also in the band, they each had two tunics – the navy blue one and a red 'festival tunic'. Someone asked –

'Is it red or blue tunics on Saturday?'

I had not even thought about it, so I asked them what they wanted to do. The discussion started mildly but threatened to become heated. Worse still, from my point of view, a lot of precious rehearsal time was being wasted. So calling a halt to the argument, I told them that they would have my decision at the end of rehearsal. Blue tunics it was, and that was that. Henceforward, no choice was offered.

On another occasion we were scheduled to go to Leeds Central Corps for a Saturday festival. It was wintertime, the route was over the Yorkshire Moors and there had been a heavy snowfall.

'Nay we can't go in this weather!' was the cry from some faint-hearts. Others were prepared to take the risk. No room for democracy here. In those days, a Saturday evening coach trip from Nelson to the Leeds pantomime was a very popular outing, so I decided that if the pantomime coaches were running on the Saturday, then we would also go to Leeds; if not, we would cancel. In the event both the pantomime and the Salvation Army coaches went over the moors to Leeds and returned to Nelson safe and sound.

I remember too the time when we were invited to be the 'Solo Brigade' at a big congressional event in Manchester. In those days, several divisions were amalgamated to form a larger unit. For Nelson Songsters this was a 'feather-in-the-cap' situation. I decided that we would sing, *I've joined the Army of the Lord*, [words: H.W. Booth, music: P. Catelinet]. Like so many songs in the present day *Salvation Army Songbook*, this was originally published for songsters: a bright, happy song, which suited us. It had three four-part (SATB) verses, each of which was followed by a catchy chorus in two parts – unison melody for the ladies and a counter-melody for the men. The piano accompaniment, played by my sister Phillis, was lively and rhythmic. The men particularly enjoyed the counter-melody, which they sang with enthusiasm and considerable flair. As we all knew this song really well, I decided that we would sing it from memory. (I have always rejected the term 'singing without music' because I have heard some choirs sing 'without music' even though they actually used their music copies). So I told the songsters – no copies. In those days this was unheard of! A short shocked silence was interrupted by a bass voice saying,

'Nay, I'm not singing 'baht' music.'

Obviously we had already tried singing it from memory and I was convinced that we would not be taking any chances on the night. So that was that. Only two copies were taken, one for the pianist and one for the conductor (just to be on the safe side).

From the start of my conducting career, I made use of any learning resource available. Nelson was the home of a renowned choir, the Nelson Arion Glee Union: at that time they were at the top of the national choral tree. How did they do it? What was the

27

secret? In an attempt to find out, I went along to one of their rehearsals – early, so as to be able to meet the conductor and ask if he would allow me to be there - his answer was the equivalent of today's 'no problem'. I have always found the experts willing to share their expertise. So from then on I went to the rehearsals whenever possible and the conductor was happy to discuss his work with me and to answer my questions. It was a valuable learning experience.

At that time there was in Nelson a nominal Salvationist who was a well-known local musician – band trainer and composer. I thought it might be useful to ask him to come to a songster practice and then to comment to me on what he had heard. This proved to be valuable: he gave me some advice that I took on board,

'Always get the sopranos to cover the high notes'.

He explained exactly what he meant and why. Since then I have tried to prevent exuberant sopranos from over-singing the high notes. Experience taught me that the higher the note, the more weight it has vis-à-vis the rest of the choir. For me, a fortissimo chord with a high soprano note needs ff from the basses but not more than mezzo-forte (if that) from the sopranos.

Music festivals, such as the ones I had attended with school choirs, were still very popular in the Lancashire/Yorkshire areas in the 1940s, so here was another source of choral education. The choir performances were always very interesting, not only for the singing, but also for the presentation and the conducting. But the most important part of the experience for me was the adjudication. I would jot down some of the things I noticed as each choir performed and then compare my notes with the adjudicator's comments. Why did some choirs get more marks than others? What was the adjudicator looking for? What were the good things about a performance and where could improvements be made? I would award a mark for each piece, and then compare it with that of the adjudicator. I was a happy lady when he agreed with me!

At my new school, as had been the case at Whitefield, there already was a music teacher: I had to take over the timetable of the person I was replacing. Once again I taught physical education (girls), but as I had been on an accredited course at Loughborough College, I felt more comfortable with the apparatus work. I thoroughly enjoyed teaching netball and was extremely gratified when my school netball team reached the final of the Lancashire Inter-school Netball Competition, playing against, and narrowly losing to Manchester High School for Girls. For their training I had formed a boys' netball team and coached the two teams together. The result was that the girls learned cunning and speed from the boys, whilst the latter learned the game itself and its tactics. The school hall was also used as a badminton court: this was my favourite game. Several of the teachers were very keen, so we formed a team to play in the Burnley, Nelson and Colne League. Later I was chosen to play for that league in the Lancashire League – the peak of my badminton career. Life was not all work and no play!

My new school timetable contained a nasty shock: as well as no music teaching, I had to teach crafts to a group of fourteen to fifteen-year-old boys. The crafts were bookbinding and cane-work (basketry). I knew absolutely nothing about either subject! Emergency action was needed. I found some books in the local library, bought the materials needed, and taught myself to bind books and weave baskets! Actually it was enjoyable. The boys were excellent workers and produced some good examples of these crafts. When, because of the limitations of the equipment available to us, we were not able to go further with bookbinding, we decided to try binding miniature books. This was a huge success and great fun. We borrowed fine thread, needles and tape from the needlework department and the boys vied with each other to produce the smallest most perfect book.

During my time at Bradley School, I had only one serious discipline problem. I was on 'dinner duty' alone: all other staff were elsewhere. A known bully indulged in some unacceptable behaviour. I told him to stay behind after he had finished his meal. Watching him out of the corner of my eye, I saw him stand up and leave the table. At that point I nonchalantly strolled to stand by the closed classroom door: he purposefully came straight towards me. There was an eye-to-eye confrontation. As with Miss L in the 'mental arithmetic' episode, I had to win. So I stood my ground and fortunately he stopped short of barging me out of the way. When no other pupil was left in the room, and after quietly explaining that his behaviour had been unacceptable, I gently opened the door and let him go. He had expected at least a verbal assault! That was a lesson for me. As he had stayed behind when he could so easily have pushed me aside, I felt that any further action on my part would be counter-productive. A 'win-win' situation had been created – the best of all resolutions of a conflict. Having learnt that lesson so early in my career, I was better equipped to deal equably with problems created by unnecessary violence (verbal) meted out by some teachers.

'I hold a number of beliefs that have been repudiated by many of the liveliest minds of our times. I believe that order is better than anarchy; creation better than destruction; I prefer gentleness to violence and forgiveness to vendetta. On the whole I think learning is preferable to ignorance and I am sure that human sympathy is better than ideology!'

Sir Kenneth Clark

Music was not on my timetable, but fortunately for me, the music teacher was quite happy for me to start a choir and equally happy to be my pianist. Although it was an extra-curricular activity, we still managed to prepare enough songs for us to be able to take part in concerts both at school and elsewhere in the town. We did a lot of carolling at Christmas-time, and sang in school carol services. But our greatest achievement was a production of a simplified version of the opera *Hansel and Gretel* by Engelbert Humperdinck – I did the music and the drama specialist was the producer.

It was at this time that my Salvation Army career and my teaching career began to move closer together. At the SA I was producing a short play – *The Stained Glass Window.* It was going quite well, but I was no drama expert: some 'finishing touches' were needed – I was powerless to supply them. So I asked the school drama teacher, who had produced *Hansel and Gretel*, if he would be willing to come to a rehearsal and do some work on the play. His ready affirmative answer meant that we had two good rehearsals with him, transforming the production from 'quite good', to 'excellent'. Much later, in the early 1960s, the National Songsters were working on a piece of music that had in it a passage of choral speaking. We did a certain amount of work on it, but I was not satisfied – it was not good enough. Some professional help in the person of Grace Catelinet, (later to become Mrs Trevor Austin) who was a well-known elocutionist and a choral-speech specialist, was at hand. Another transformation took place!

Whilst at Bradley School I went to the Royal Academy of Music for a course in music education. It was a chance remark from a young man on the course that prompted me to ask him,

'Are you a Salvationist?'

And so I met Bandmaster Don Osgood and a friendship was formed that lasted until his premature death. We worked together at Music Schools and met quite often at Salvation Army events. Then a significant event occurred. One Saturday evening, Manchester Openshaw Songsters, with their distinguished leader Harry Salthouse, were coming to share a partnership festival with Nelson Songsters. I told my school choir about this, and said that anyone could come. Three girls came, and one of them was a 14-year-old named Joyce Blackburn. On the Monday at school they sought me out to tell me that they had enjoyed the concert.

'Did you like the choir from Manchester?' I asked.

'Yes, but it was not as good as yours.'

That was a very supportive comment from them, but their judgement was probably somewhat clouded by the fact that I was their schoolteacher. However, Joyce said,

'I'd like to join your choir.'

Of course explanations were needed, especially the fact that only Salvationists could join.

'I'll be a Salvationist then,' said Joyce.

So then there were more explanations about being a soldier and wearing uniform.

'I'll become a soldier,' was Joyce's response.

So, although only 14 years old, that is exactly what she did, with very little support from home, but no outright opposition. She had thought that as soon as she was made a soldier, she could join the songsters. The fact was that fifteen years was the age at Nelson at that time for new members to start attending practices. She pleaded with me and I said that as soon as she became fifteen she could come to practices.

One Wednesday at school she came to me with the same old question; could she come to songster practice that night.

'Joyce, you know you can't come until you are fifteen.'

With a big smile she replied, 'I'm fifteen today!'

Joyce had a beautiful singing voice. She went to the first 'singing company camp' at Sunbury Court in 1948, and sang a solo at Chalk Farm on the Sunday at the end of the week. She eventually married Laurence Coupland, a bandsman at Doncaster Corps. We kept in touch and met occasionally over the years. Later, with her husband and two sons, she emigrated to Canada. Today she is still singing as a valued member of Edmonton Songsters. It was my great pleasure to visit her in 1999 and it was a joy to hear her, in the Sunday morning meeting at Edmonton, singing a song which I had taught her many, many years before: Ernest Rance's *Lovest thou Me?*

Just as learning to make baskets and binding books had been a matter of urgency, so it was with learning to be a choral director. I was having to learn very quickly the skills of training and conducting a choir. 'In at the deep end' is an appropriate metaphor for a new songster leader. When I had an opportunity to go to a 'choral training' day under the tutelage of Hubert Bardgett, the renowned chorus master of the then famous, and still famous, Huddersfield Choral Society, I jumped at the chance. On such courses there is usually an opportunity for the students to conduct the group. I was one of the volunteers to do this; it presented a unique opportunity for my choral conducting to be appraised by one of the top men in the business. I remember there were some comments of approval and that the criticisms were kindly presented as suggestions. It was an experience that spurred me on to learn all I could about being a choral director. During that time I gathered together a selection of books on the subject of choral conducting. Leslie Woodgate, Joseph Lewis and Sir Adrian Bolt were just a few of the authors. In the songster room we kept a small library of books on singing which could be borrowed. Some keen songsters read them all, some read a few, and others none at all. The importance lay in the fact that the books were there and available.

Over the years I have maintained my interest in education for choral directors, and have found that there are common elements in all forms of music making. A cello master class on TV with Paul Tortelier can be as enlightening as a drama master class with Janet Suzman or a percussion master class with Evelyn Glennie. On one occasion, an outstanding young 'cellist was playing for Paul Tortelier; he commended her on her beautiful performance, but, (isn't there always a 'but'?)

> 'Sometimes you try to persuade me too much,' he
> told her.

That can happen in all kinds of music making and especially in the choral world. When I saw Janet Suzman on TV with a group of drama students reading a conversation from a Shakespearean play, it was rather dull. Then she gave them a modern scenario in a similar context and told them (about five of them) to improvise. Well, they really had a go and became very animated. Then it was back to Shakespeare, which miraculously had now come to life. At a Southampton Divisional Music School a similar thing happened. I had chosen Eric Ball's *Pilgrim Song* for the whole school to sing together. Some people expressed their doubts about its suitability for teenagers.

'Wait and see,' was my reply.

The actual music is ideal for teenage voices: some SATB work, with a really interesting bass part, some unison and each verse with a piano introduction. There are four whole bars of four-part work with no accompaniment. The students soon learnt it and appeared to like it but in my view it had not yet come alive. Something had to be done. I asked one of the older girls to paraphrase John Bunyan's words into modern 20th century English. At the next rehearsal she read out her paraphrase (which I had already vetted) and then they sang. What a difference: they now sang with imagination and conviction! They sang the notes, they sang the words but now they made it come alive. The final 'I'll labour night and day to be a Pilgrim' was utterly convincing. Eric Ball would have approved.

We sometimes listen to a choir which is singing with accuracy; the pitch, the words, the notes, the volume and changes thereof – all correct. They are reproducing in sound what is actually written on the copy. But they are NOT making music nor are they communicating. I have often said in rehearsal,

'Turn the notes into music, and the words into thoughts.'

Communication and imagination are both essential in good choral singing. The music and the words must come alive! Recently I read,

'When rehearsing for a performance of Messiah, Beecham stopped the proceedings and addressed the choir: "When we sing *All we like sheep have gone astray,* might we have a little more regret and a little less satisfaction"?'

The advent of TV has given today's choral enthusiasts the opportunity not only to hear, but also to see top-class soloists and choirs. 'The Sainsbury Choir of the Year' – a biennial event – should be watched by all choralists and conductors. Music festivals, like those of my early days in Lancashire are still part of the choral life of this country: any aspiring choral conductor would benefit from attending some of these, as I discovered for myself in the late 1940s. Once again, the commentaries are extremely interesting and enlightening. Two other superb TV programmes are the 'Cardiff Singer of the World' and the 'Young Musician of the Year'. In these days of advanced technology, it is easy to record such programmes for later study.

The formation of the Association of British Choral Directors (ABCD) in the mid-eighties (20th Century) created a wonderful learning resource for choral directors – there was nothing like this in my early days as a songster leader. From small beginnings it has grown into a huge enterprise with regional groups in most parts of the country. On the first Tuesday in July, there is an annual 'singposium' at the South Bank in London, co-existing with the choir day of the annual 'Music for Youth' week at the same venue. Each year, an increasing number of Salvationists can be found at this event, which for us becomes a social occasion as well as a learning experience. Then on the August Bank Holiday weekend, the association organises a massive convention, which is held at a different location each year. Additionally, many regional branches arrange choral days and workshops. Recently a few of us from Staines Corps went to a 'Singing with John Rutter' day in Sevenoaks – it was fantastic! After the inevitable and very fashionable 'warm-ups', he gave us an excellent demonstration of how to conduct a rehearsal – to keep it moving along, to maintain the choir's interest and to achieve music-making of a high standard.

In 1947 there was much publicity in the SA literature about the first 'YP Band Music Camp', although I learn that in 1929 and in subsequent years, band camps were organized by the National Young People's Department. The 1939-1945 war put a stop to these activities, and it was not until 1947 that a new series of 'band camps' was inaugurated. In 1948 an advert in *The Bandsman and Songster* advertised a second such 'camp'. Immediately, the question arose in my mind, 'What about the singing companies?' The British Commissioner of that time was Commissioner William Dalziel, and I had a question to ask him.

'What are you going to do for the singing companies?' I wrote to him, the first of many letters.

They had no plans.

'Why not?' I wanted to know.

'Perhaps next year', was the reply.

Not good enough. 'Why not this year?'

'Too late to organize'.

I wrote back with some suggestions to counter the 'too late' argument. It must have cost me a small fortune in stamps, but it was worth it. Commissioner Dalziel capitulated and the first 'singing company camp' was held at Sunbury Court in 1948. I was invited to attend this ground-breaking event as a tutor. School holidays in Nelson were different from those in most parts of the country and I would be teaching at school on the music camp dates. An application for 'leave of absence' was granted without salary. This was a financial blow; I thought and hoped that my travelling expenses would be reimbursed, as indeed they were. It was my first visit to Sunbury Court and now I live just round the corner from it. It was at this inaugural 'music camp for girls' that I met so many well-known Salvationist musicians who at that time were just names to me - Songster Leader Brindley Boon, Major Wesley Evans, Major Hiscock, Songster Leader Sam Hooper, Major Ivy Mawby and Colonel K. Westergaard. The whole week was just an 'out-of-this-world' experience for a young songster leader from a small corps in Lancashire. *Such a Lovely World He Made* [words: Doris Rendell, music: Brindley Boon], the favourite song at that first school, was sung again at the Adult Music School (2003) when Brindley was a visiting guest. He conducted us and it was an unforgettable experience.

Colonel K. Westergaard was the officer in charge of the 1948 'music camp'. In conversation he commented that it was fortunate that the event coincided with school holidays.

'Not so in Nelson' I replied.

'How is that?'

'Nelson's holidays are three weeks in July and then we have another two weeks in September. This goes back to the times when help was needed in the fields for the harvest.'

'Are they paying your salary for the week?'

'I'm afraid not.'

'How much is a week's salary?'

'Six pounds,'

Later in the day I was given a cheque for six pounds and a receipt for me to sign. It was very caring of Colonel Westergaard to reimburse me for lost salary. That was not the end of it. At home, a letter from the education authority was waiting for me: would I do a week's supervision at the 'camp school' in September? If so, my salary would be re-instated. I had previously spent a week at the camp school and loved it – right out in the country near the local landmark – Pendle Hill. The offer was accepted and the cheque returned to Colonel Westergaard!

Thus did the music school movement start in this country. After years of development we now have a programme of mixed schools, both national and divisional, almost all of which have on their syllabus mixed voice singing where everybody joins in (including all members of staff, I hope!). This is something for which I lobbied. When in 1982 Colonel Norman Bearcroft invited me to the Territorial Music School, I had a condition: I would be happy to go if at some point in the daily programme singing by the whole school would be featured. Norman seemed a bit doubtful, then he said,

'Well, you'll have to do it yourself.'

'All right, I'll do it.'

So for the first time at the Territorial Music School, a mixed voice chorus had a rehearsal scheduled on the daily programme. Colonel Ray Steadman-Allan wrote something special for us: *This Age of Rockets*. It was just the sort of thing to appeal to the young musicians. The text [words: J. Izzard] set to original music, explored the concept of *This Age of Rockets*, but finished with a setting of words by Frances Ridley Havergal to the glorious tune *Rachie*. With a stirring brass and percussion accompaniment it made a most moving finale as the students sang:

'By Thy grand redemption,
By Thy Grace Divine,
We are on the Lord's side,
Saviour, we are Thine'.

The singing was both a testimony and a challenge – utterly convincing.

When at a later date I went to do the singing at the Swedish Music School, I introduced *This Age of Rockets* to the young people there, with the same compelling message, and when the Hendon Songsters sang it one Sunday afternoon on an 'away' weekend, a young lady made her way to the mercy seat during the singing of that last movement,-

'Master, Thou wilt keep us
by Thy Grace Divine,
Always on the Lord's side,
Saviour, always Thine'.

It is a powerful song, but sadly it has never been published.

For me, involvement with Salvation Army Choral Work at National level started at that first 'singing company camp' for girls at Sunbury Court. I could not have imagined at that time where it would lead nor how long it would last.

CHAPTER FOUR
'Serve the Lord with gladness,
come before his presence with singing'.
(Psalm 100:2)

My move from Nelson to Luton was the end of the beginning: from a small cotton weaving town to a large motor-manufacturing area, where the economy was dependent on the Vauxhall Motor Company: from the Salvation Army Corps where I had grown up to Luton Citadel where initially I knew only four people, and from a large involvement in SA activities – mostly music – to being a member of a songster brigade.

During the war years and up to 1950, Phillis and I had somehow become known as 'The Wilson Sisters'. Wartime restrictions, including depletion of bands and songsters due to mobilization, meant that small groups of salvationist musicians emerged and it was they mostly who did the 'specialling'. Isabel Stoker (elocution) and Iris Claxton (piano) were very well known. Majors George Wood and Eric Russell, leaders of small groups, travelled throughout the country during the War years. In an article which appeared in *The Musician* on the 13th October 1984, Colonel Brindley Boon wrote:

> 'Muriel Wilson, a product of the Lancashire Corps of Nelson, began to attract the attention of discerning Salvationists beyond her local environs, when, with her songster leader father and her sister Phillis, she became a popular visitor for weekend campaigns. Although this happened in the frustrating 'blackout' days of the Second World War, the family trio made its mark with items expertly presented on a variety of instruments – banjolin, cornet and piano among them'.

At this time a Major Portas was stationed at Nelson: his son Walter, a lieutenant, visited his parents; he must have heard us making music. At any rate, he invited us as a family – mother came too – to go to his corps in Lincolnshire for a weekend. With my dad, we could muster quite a variety of items:

Songster Leader Wilson – tenor and cornet soloist,

Phillis Wilson – piano, accordion, vocal,

Muriel Wilson – piano, banjolin, vocal.

The possibilities of 'mix and match' were numerous. Vocal solos and duets, piano solos and duets, accordion solos, banjolin solos, accordion and banjolin duets, sometimes with vocal added, and any mix of the above as trios. My dad was the leader of the group taking responsibility for the Sunday meetings.

After this we were invited to Scunthorpe for a weekend. How this came about I am not sure, but I believe that Bandmaster Whitby, of Scunthorpe, had heard us on our visit to the Lincolnshire Corps. Phillis and I stayed at the bandmaster's home, which was a very 'good billet'. The two families formed a friendship that lasted for many years. When my sister married Tony Metcalf, Bandmaster Whitby officiated at the wedding in what would have been my father's place, 'giving the bride away'.

In this twenty-first century we rarely have a 'chairman' to preside over a musical festival; very often the participants or leaders of sections introduce the items. On the Saturday evening at Scunthorpe, the chairman was the owner of THE jewellery shop in the town. After the meeting, he invited Phillis and me to go to look at his shop – he was most insistent! It was a very up-market emporium, not the sort of place we were used to! To our surprise he said,

'Now, I'd like you to choose something for yourselves.'

We looked at each other in amazement. Phillis said,

'Oh no, we couldn't do that.'

'Yes, I insist – just choose something,' he replied.

What a temptation – silver, gold, precious stones, the like of which was way beyond anything we could possibly afford to buy! So we looked around for something that was not an expensive item. I settled for a small clock, and Phillis chose the least expensive brooch she could find.

In 1940 we met Maisie Ringham (now Wiggins). Whilst still a schoolgirl she came to Nelson Corps with her father and billeted with us. A report of the event in *The Bandsman and Songster* reads:

> 'Nelson Band (Townsley) and Songsters (Wilson) assisted Young People's Bandmember Maisie Ringham (trombone) in a programme in which Songster Phyllis Wilson provided pianoforte accompaniments. Lt-Col Greenaway, who was captain in charge of Nelson Corps fifty-three years ago, and formed the band there, supported his trombonist granddaughter'.
>
> V. Packham (Jun.)

Today (2003) Maisie, still playing her trombone in Staines band, teaches both at 'The Harrow School' and privately, and worships with her husband Ray at Staines Corps; we see each other regularly. Many young and aspiring brass players at the Corps have benefited from her professional tuition – do they realize how fortunate they are, I wonder? Back in the '40s, Maisie often joined Phillis and me on our 'weekends away', bringing true professionalism to the group. My contribution was the least in a musical sense, although people seemed to like hearing my banjolin. Phillis was always Maisie's accompanist when we teamed up for 'specialling'. Her first professional orchestral engagement was with the Wessex Orchestra: it happened to be in Colne – next door neighbour to Nelson. Maisie arranged to stay with us, but she had an urgent problem. Professional female musicians were expected to wear long black, or nearly black, dresses for performances. Maisie didn't have one.

'Muriel, have you got anything to lend me?'

'My only long dress is a dark midnight blue. Let's see what you think.'

The dress was just right. I lent her a lovely chain necklace to go with it. Maisie liked them so much that she kept them – a fact of which she recently reminded me. At that time, her need was greater than mine!

Since then, we have kept in touch and worked together from time to time. Two never-to-be-forgotten occasions occurred when Maisie was stranded without her usual pianist – her sister-in-law, Marjorie Ringham; in desperation she asked me if I could help her out. It involved a Saturday evening at Staines and later a weekend at Plymouth Congress Hall. I was by no means in the Phillis Metcalf/Marjorie Ringham class as an accompanist. My only advantage was knowing most of Maisie's solo repertoire and being a good music sight-reader. The Staines engagement was an absolute horror to me. At the time there was an epidemic of typhoid in Wales where the National Songsters were soon to go. We all had to be vaccinated: for me, it was just before the visit to Staines. Saying 'yes' to Maisie had committed me to a lot of piano practice. After the injection, my right arm got steadily worse – swelling, burning and throbbing. I remember with great clarity that drive from Eastcote to and from Staines and the tremendous discomfort that I suffered all evening. Driving home was a nightmare; on arrival, I went straight upstairs and collapsed on the bed! The weekend at Plymouth Congress Hall was much less stressful as I was familiar with most of the accompaniments. However, accompanying a professional such as Maisie was never completely stress-free for me: it seemed to be a long weekend.

Weekends away are part of the Salvation Army music scene. Nelson Songsters' first such weekend was when we were invited to Scunthorpe soon after I became the songster leader. This was followed by a weekend at Rochdale. I am sure that many Salvationists remember such weekends away by the 'billets' they had. At Rochdale on the Saturday evening, when I arrived at my 'billet', I was shown into a smoky room where four men were absorbed in a game of cards, their table lit by a pendant lamp which was the only light in the room. So I sat alone on the one chair available and waited. The lady of the house came in,

'Would you like a cup of tea?'

'Yes please. I'd like that,' I replied.

The tea was brought and then my hostess left the room. She came back later to say, 'I'll show you to your room now.'

'Thank you.'

That was that, and I was hungry!

I think that someone ought to collect anecdotes of billeting experiences with a view to putting them into a book: it would probably be a Salvation Army best-seller!

When at a later date Vic and I went to Maisie's corps for her band weekend, we stayed with a lovely man who was a retired batman to an RAF officer. He treated us in exactly the same way he was used to treating his RAF officers. We were called to a beautifully-laid table, our host would then doff his cap, say grace, and replacing his cap, would serve us and leave us. It was a unique experience. More was to come! On the dressing-table in the bedroom were some beautiful crochet mats. In the morning, I commented on the mats – just a conversation point.

'Do you like them?' our host asked.

'I think they are lovely,' I replied.

'I made them myself.'

'Did you? That's wonderful.'

'You shall have them. I'll give them to you.'

'Oh no! You mustn't do that.' But he did.

At lunchtime, there was a beautiful vase of roses in the centre of the table. Naturally I commented, 'The roses are beautiful.'

'You shall have them,' he replied.

'Oh no! You must keep them yourself.'

'Yes, I shall give them to you after the meeting tonight.'

After tea, Vic and I were sitting in the lounge. We had not been married long: we lived in rented accommodation, and only had the bare necessities. As we sat there, I said to Vic,

'Isn't this a lovely rug?'

'DON'T MENTION IT' was the brusque and firm reply. 'If you say anything, he'll roll it up and give it to you, then I'll have to fasten it on the roof of the car to take it home.' (It was a large rug.) I didn't mention it!

Once I had become songster leader at Nelson, I had my first experience of planning special weekends at the corps. Soon after my 1948 week at the singing company camp, I invited Major Wesley Evans and Songster Leader Brindley Boon to come and conduct the songster weekend. At that time, both these men were writing for songster brigades and it was a lovely thrill for the members of this provincial brigade to meet in the flesh, the composers whose names were already familiar to them, and whose music they were singing. Brindley and Wesley stayed at my home, and on the Sunday, I invited our commanding officers to come for tea. During conversation after tea, the commanding officer's wife took out her autograph album and handed it to Wesley: would he please sign it? He was happy to do so, after which he was passing it to Brindley, when the lady reached out and snatched it back,

'That's for officers only!' was her somewhat stern comment.

I wonder if, later, when Brindley became an officer she regretted not having his autograph in her precious book?

For some of my special Saturday evening festivals I would try to get a local celebrity to chair the meeting. Learie Constantine, the great West Indian cricket all-rounder, was the Nelson professional for many years. We had met when I worked in the mill office as he was a close friend of my boss. I was invited to social occasions when I was just in my teens. Later, when I was teaching, I was asked to coach his daughter for her 11+ exams. When he was playing for the West Indies at Sheffield during my college days, he arranged for me to spend a day at the cricket ground – a lovely experience. I was a VIP for a day! So it was not surprising that I managed to get him to the Salvation Army to preside over a songster programme. The hall was packed out. Much later, when I was a senior mistress at the Manor School, Ruislip, he came as a guest speaker at speech day. At that time he was the High Commissioner for Trinidad and Tobago and arrived at the school in his official chauffeur-driven car. He was dressed in an ordinary suit, with an ordinary tie and a V-neck sweater, but as soon as he began to speak he became extra-ordinary. At an even later date he agreed to come to Northwood School to be the guest at the speech day, but, unfortunately the Government sent him to Africa on a delicate diplomatic mission. However, he arranged for his wife, Gloria, to come in his stead. She was a lovely lady whose presence enhanced the occasion.

I am sure that all Salvationists who go 'specialling' can recall numerous travelling problems and mishaps. One day we were booked to go to Barnoldswick, about 15 miles from Nelson. It was before the end of the war, therefore 'blackout' restrictions were in operation. On this occasion Maisie brought with her Major Grace Rolls, a lovely soprano singer, (wife of Douglas Rolls). Vic was also coming with us as he was home on leave from the RAF. We hired a cab – none of us had cars in those days - and set out through the countryside to that small corps. Suddenly a thick fog descended and the driver was forced to reduce speed. The cumulative effect of the blackout - including the ban on the use of headlights - and the fog, meant that our speed was reduced to a crawl. The driver then came to a halt in a farmyard – we were completely off the beaten track. The farmer came out of his house, holding a hooded lantern on a stick! He told us to turn round, go up the hill and turn right at the top to get back on the road for Barnoldswick. The only safe way to do this was for Vic to walk just in front of the vehicle until we were safely back on the main road again, which was only a 'B' road anyway! Eventually we reached Barnoldswick and found the hall.

We expected to see it empty and in darkness, but no! As we went up the steps to the meeting room, we heard singing, the sound of timbrels and clapping. There they all were, having a jolly good time, waiting for the 'specials'. We could do no other than give them the whole planned programme, which did not end until 10.40 pm. Our efforts were rewarded however, not just by their enthusiastic reception, thanks, and the lovely refreshments provided in spite of stringent rationing. No! The bonus was that when we looked out of the hall door, the fog had disappeared and the moon was shining brightly. We felt that 'Someone' was pleased with our efforts.

A very special visitor to our home during the war was a sergeant in the Royal Canadian Army: Eric Sharpe from Danforth Corps. He was travelling about the country on extended 'leave', visiting various corps where he charmed everybody with his beautiful tenor voice. Not only had he a lovely voice, but he also knew how to use it. The two things do not necessarily go together. This started a life-long friendship: we met whenever he was in this country, and visited him in his home in Canada. He brought the Danforth Songster Brigade on a UK tour and visited us on other occasions. Hendon Songsters enjoyed his visit to the songster practice where I invited him to do some choral work with us.

In 1945 my sister married Tony Metcalf; not only was he an excellent trombonist, but he also had a good baritone voice. Vic, who was later to become my husband, had a lovely tenor voice, so when eventually they both returned from the 'Forces', we became an SATB quartet. For me the bonus was that both those men were keen on being in the songster brigade. The four of us were invited to go to Jersey for a special weekend: our previous Officers, Major and Mrs H. Hales, were stationed at St. Helier Corps. We had it all planned, but then my mother went into hospital for surgery. I was the most expendable member of the group and was happy to stay behind to look after her. This was the time when, for me, family came first.

When I left Nelson in 1950 I could not possibly have imagined what would happen to me in the future as a salvationist musician and as a teacher. In response to requests, I had already started writing articles in *The Bandsman and Songster* weekly paper, had been a tutor at the National Music School for Girls (YP Singing Company Camp in those days), and for five years I had been a songster leader. Arriving in Luton, I acquired a new name, I had a new home (albeit rented), a new corps and songster brigade, and a new school – anything could happen!

CHAPTER FIVE
'In all thy ways acknowledge Him
and He shall direct your paths'.
(Proverbs 3:6)

In 1950 some wartime austerities remained – food rationing was still in force, utility furniture was the 'norm', but clothing coupons were no longer needed. We were still in the 'make-do-and-mend' mode, and for Vic and me, money was scarce. Financially, our number-one priority was to save up enough money for a deposit on a house. In the meantime we rented two rooms in a small semi-detached house, sharing a bathroom and kitchen. I remember the first Sunday in our new home. The previous day I had made an apple pie for Sunday lunch. As there was no refrigerator, I did as my mother used to do and popped it in the cold oven until the next day. When I went to get it out, I found that it was already half-eaten – mice had got at it! The remnants went into the bin. I squirm now at the thought of it! Vic dealt with the problem and made the kitchen into a mouse-free zone. To our amazement, the owners were not too pleased!

Not realizing that Luton had its own local education authority, I had applied to Bedfordshire for a teaching post. My appointment was to a one-form entry secondary school in Toddington – way out in the countryside. There was no easy way of getting there: our only means of transport was two bicycles and public transport – otherwise we walked. To get to Toddington I had to walk one mile to catch the hourly bus. The 8.30 am was too late for me, so it was necessary to leave home just after 7 am. The return journey was equally inconvenient. Throughout my career, being early for work was very important to me whether it be at school or at Salvation Army events where I had some responsibility. I couldn't bear to be late. During that autumn term I tried an interesting mode of transport. My husband taught at a school that was almost on my bus route. He cycled to school so I started to cycle with him; at his school I then left my bicycle and got a lift on a motorbike to Toddington. The young motorcyclist taught at Toddington Junior School; his friend taught at the same school as Vic, so we did a switch. The system worked well both to and from school. However, the motorcycle's rattle got progressively worse and I jokingly predicted that one day the engine would fall off. One morning it almost did! At any rate, it slipped out of position with a big bang and that was the end of that! I had to help push the wretched thing up the hill into Toddington and much to my chagrin, arrived late at school – the first time ever! So it was back to the 7.30 am bus, with the thought coming into my head that I really ought to try to get a job in Luton.

Toddington was a very pleasant school in which to teach; there were only five full-time teaching staff besides the head teacher, a retired army major (HM Forces), two part-time teachers and the usual ancillary staff, including a fantastic cook who, on the premises, made us the best school meals I have ever tasted! It was real 'home' cooking. Another bonus was the fire stove in each classroom; it was a cold winter (I noticed that, waiting for the early morning bus) and the lovely warmth of the classroom was most comforting. No needlework this time! A Mrs Shaw, a retired head teacher came in part time for that. My timetable was English, maths, some physical education and some music.

I learned a big lesson from Mrs Shaw. One day a boy persisted in reading a comic when he should have been doing something else. After a few warnings, I confiscated his comic, and later burnt it in the corner stove in my class room. That, I thought, was that. But no! He asked me for it, and I fobbed him off. Then again – the same, after which he said that his dad would be coming for his comic. Time to ask Mrs Shaw for advice.

'What shall I do now?' I asked.

'Set him on looking for it' she replied. 'Let him have a friend to help him. They can tidy up your shelves and bookcase at the same time. Let them stay in the classroom at break and dinner times, they will like that.'

So I took her advice, and the outcome was very tidy shelves and cupboards: no more was heard about the comic. Ever after that, I kept all confiscated items, and promised they would be returned to any parent who liked to come for them. As a result, when I retired some thirty years later, my desk drawer was full of odds and ends, including a fairly valuable stock of cigarettes.

Then there was a boy called Billy. He was always talking, thus didn't do much work. Although he was intelligent, 'Could do better' would have been an appropriate comment on his report. One day I decided to send him to the head teacher for not working. When he returned, his face was white, perspiration stood on his forehead and he seemed absolutely petrified. That worried me. What had happened to him? Surely he hadn't been beaten? At the first opportunity I went to see the head teacher.

'I'm worried about Billy,' I said.

'Oh, what's the problem?'

'I didn't send him to you to be caned.'

'Well, I didn't cane him.'

'Please tell me what happened!'

'Nothing! I just showed him the cane and said that that was what he would get if he were sent to me again,' .

Obviously, the sight of the cane in the hands of a six-foot former military Major was too much for Billy; he learnt his lesson.

Early in my teaching career I had realised that no two schools are alike. In Nelson, Whitefield was my most unpleasant teaching experience and Bradley was an absolute haven of peace by comparison. Now I had found a lovely little school and a comfortable job in Toddington. The only friction revealed itself from time to time when the staff were having lunch together. Suddenly the head teacher, a true blue Tory, would get up and walk out of the room without finishing his lunch or making a comment. After this had happened several times, I needed Mrs Shaw again.

'Why does the head suddenly get up from his unfinished meal, and just walk out of the room?'

'Because he cannot stand Mr G any longer.'

Apparently Mr G was a red-hot communist, to whom Mr Y had become allergic.

A young geography teacher was in his first year of teaching. Toddington, being a small school, meant that his noisy class could be heard in most areas of the school building. I asked Mrs Shaw if she knew what was going on.

'Oh, it's the new-fangled teaching methods that they learn in College these days. The problem is, in his first year of teaching, he does not have the class-management skills to cope with these new ways of doing things, and when he gets enough experience, he'll have more sense!'

I was enjoying being at Toddington School – it was pleasantly peaceful. But the journey! My reluctant decision that it was too much, led me to apply to Luton Education Authority for a teaching post. Almost immediately they interviewed me for a job at a girls' school in Stopsley on the outskirts of Luton. I was pleased to accept, especially as teaching in a girls' school would be a new experience. Unfortunately, the school was just about as far from where I lived as any Luton school could be. The buses were quite frequent however and the walk to the bus stop was reasonably short.

Meanwhile, I had settled into Luton Citadel Songsters. Hubert Janes, the songster leader, and his wife, Iris, became our very good friends. They were exceptionally kind to this rather impecunious couple; many happy hours were spent in their home. We also had some wonderful friends from my Nelson days in the corps: Vic had lived with Harry and Miriam Pickup before we were married and their daughter, Kathleen, had been my bridesmaid. They continued to care for us, welcoming us into their family. So, for me, Luton was a happy place. We were also invited to join a small group of singers who called themselves 'The Occasional Singers'. Although we had a weekly rehearsal, performances really were 'occasional'. We sang a lot of unaccompanied madrigals and motets: I liked that. Some of this music was useful to me later when I was in charge of music at a school in Ruislip. The opportunity to be part of singing groups again proved to be a great learning experience.

At Toddington I had taught very little music, but all hopes of music at Stopsley were dashed. Before the start of term (January 1951), the head teacher invited me to her home for coffee. However, it transpired that the real purpose was to tell me that, although I was a qualified music teacher, there would be no music on my timetable as there already was a musician on the staff. She also expressed the hope that there would not be 'any trouble'. I assured her that if there were, it would not be of my making. So once again I was to take over the timetable of the teacher I was replacing: English, maths, and needlework. For the next two terms, playing the piano for some less than enthusiastic and somewhat chaotic hymn practices was the only music in which I was involved. Two books would be on my piano music stand: the hymnbook and a reading book. I read my book, whilst at the same time listening out for the moment when my skills at the piano would be required.

Fortunately for me, the music teacher soon moved away and I was asked to take over. Of course I needed to see the music syllabus, according to which the school had a choir and an orchestra, neither of which were actually in existence. The head teacher agreed to my rewriting the syllabus which I made challenging but realistic: I ensured that what I included was achievable. For the first time in my career, I was teaching my favourite subject throughout the school and could do it my way.

Stopsley School was built on a large site and housed two separate schools: one for boys and the girls' school. A large assembly hall was shared by the two schools. I soon got to know the music master of the boys' school; he was the organist and choirmaster at the Luton Parish Church. Once I had got my work organised and moving along smoothly, I suggested that we could perhaps have a mixed choir occasionally. This was before the raising of the school-leaving age, so the oldest pupils were fifteen. There was no sixth form, so it didn't seem possible to do soprano, alto, tenor and bass work. Nevertheless we did join up – at least, his boys came to me: I rather think he chose to miss this after-school activity. He seemed a bit apprehensive about the behaviour of his boys and asked me to report any misbehaviour to him – the culprits would be punished. I was not expecting to have, nor did I have any problems, but I was curious. What would the punishment be? I had visions of canes, straps, or even worse. So I asked,

'How will you punish them?'

'No more weddings' was the quick, and to him the obvious reply. Apparently many of the choir boys at school were also in his church choir and for these boys, a wedding was a lucrative event!

It was at this point in my teaching career that I began to invite musician friends to come to the school to give recitals. As a Salvationist, I had a lot of contacts. In those days the non-Grammar Schools were not bedevilled with the stresses of external examinations, so there could be some flexibility in the school timetable. Margaret Veal, a Welsh Salvationist studying piano in London, was very willing to come to give a recital. She suggested that she should bring a friend who was studying singing. When offered the opportunity of having them perform to the boys, Mr Dawes, the head teacher, enthusiastically accepted, and so it was arranged, - girls first, boys second. These two students really were good, giving an excellent programme: well chosen, well performed and enthusiastically received. At the end of the second performance, Mr Dawes stood at the hall door, smiling and speaking to his boys as they filed out and I overheard the following conversation:

'Well Johnny, did you enjoy the concert?'

(Johnny was a big and rather rough-looking young man.)

'Yes, sir' (enthusiastically).

'Which piece did you like best?'

'The one that played the piano, sir!'

(With a broad grin).

So much for the music!

My next innovation was to have a one-day music festival when each class would sing two prepared songs to the rest of the school. The head teacher was very supportive of this event, agreeing immediately to suspend the school timetable for the day. The rest of the staff were delighted – a day off from teaching. As I was teaching music to all eight classes, whatever competition was engendered would be fair. That the girls would be able to hear the work of other classes was one of the aims of the event. It was very interesting for me to prepare sixteen songs with enough variety to hold the listeners' attention. An adjudicator was needed – someone who could spend the day at the school, give informed and enlightened comments about the performances and generally be an encourager. My first and VIP choice was Eric Ball, whom I had recently met and who had started writing and arranging songs for the Salvation Army music schools with which I was involved. I was delighted when he agreed to come: a date was fixed and preparations were begun: I was looking forward to having Eric at the school for the whole day.

He was picked up at Luton station and brought to the school. I arranged for the head teacher to bring him into the school hall where we were all assembled, and as he walked in, the whole school sang in unison, his own setting of *He who would valiant be*. It was a wonderful day: Eric captivated the girls as he spoke to them from the piano, playing to illustrate his points. There was no actual adjudication: it was officially not a competition, although in reality they all wanted to win! Eric commented on each group's songs, giving commendation and encouragement.

The school choir sang two of his songs, and at my request, he commented fully on the performance. He was well pleased. As he left the hall, once again the whole school sang *He who would valiant be*. That day was one of the most memorable of my whole teaching career.

Competitive music festivals were a feature of my own school days and throughout my career I occasionally entered a choir for such festivals. I decided that my Stopsley girls should be given the challenge and this was to be my own first experience of competitive singing as a conductor: (we don't have competitive festivals in the Salvation Army do we?) I remember taking a young colleague to a Salvation Army band festival featuring three bands, including Hendon.

'Is it a competition?' she asked.

'No' was my reply, 'but Hendon is going to win!'

When I told my girls that we were to enter a competition, they were quite excited but a bit apprehensive as I was. However, some of them were used to the big occasion, as they belonged to the then famous Luton Girls' Choir. At that time the Balham & Tooting Festival had a reputation for high standards, so we entered the school choir class. We were required to sing two songs, a set piece and an own choice. My choice was a two - part setting for ladies voices of Wordsworth's poem *To Daffodils* by Eric Thiman, a well-known organist and composer. He had given the song the title, *I wandered lonely as a cloud*. It is my all-time favourite two-part song for female voices, with a beautiful piano accompaniment. Our pianist was a former pupil of the school who was not only a good pianist, but was also a superb accompanist – the two things do not always go together.

One day, shortly before the competition, a retired music teacher friend of the head teacher was visiting the school. As I always welcome an independent informed opinion of my work, she was invited to come and listen to us rehearsing. So we sang for her. We sang about the daffodils, and as I write this, some fifty years later, I can hear the song the whole way through and even now 'My heart with pleasure fills and dances with the daffodils'. When the song ended, I went to our listeners for the visitor's verdict. It was a very short one.

'My dear,' said the lady, 'I could see the daffodils.'

About a week before the event, I once again read the syllabus to make sure I had got everything just right. For the first time I actually looked – quite casually – to see who was adjudicating. To my horror I saw that it was Eric Thiman, the composer of my own choice. What a foolhardy thing to do! Why hadn't I checked sooner? It was too late to make a change. I would try to forget about it and press on with the preparation. There was no need for the girls to know what had happened: time enough for them to be told after the event. It was quite nerve-racking – the important thing for me was not to show it. That had to be my attitude throughout all the years that I was involved in choral conducting. I never completely lost my initial nervousness, but it was essential not to communicate it to the members of the choir. The conductor alone is responsible for the performance – no one else can be blamed if things go astray.

We listened to the other choirs, and when it was our turn, we did our very best. At such moments, if the work has been well prepared, the main task of the conductor is to inspire the choir to sing better than they have ever previously sung. Adjudication at a competitive festival is always a tense time for the competitors. I remember in great detail what Eric Thiman said about our 'own choice' song.

'Now we come to this choir's own choice. They did a very dangerous thing – they chose to sing a song composed by the adjudicator. Fortunately for them, I liked it.'

I don't think my sigh of relief was audible, but the choir's jubilation when the marks were read out was ecstatic, - we had won the cup!

One of my conducting nightmares occurred many years later when I was conducting the Hendon Songsters at St. Albans, We were singing Ray Steadman-Allen's *Childhood Suite* – with piano, percussion and flute. In the last movement there are four bars rest for the voices whilst the accompaniment continues. After the singers join in again, that section is repeated but with only two bars rest. I had a moment of madness and failed to bring the singers in after the two bars. Elaine Cobb (piano), Elizabeth Renshaw (flute) and Nigel Charman (percussion) gamely continued playing whilst I 'mouthed' to the Songsters, 'I'm lost.' They had already got the message, and within seconds by means of telepathy and the 'oneness' of the group, they all came in together; breathing a sigh of relief, I once again took control!

It was in 1951, whilst I was at Luton Citadel Corps and Stopsley School that I became involved with a group of young songsters and older singing company members, later to be known as the 'London Girl Singers'. They were drawn from the four London Divisions. At that time, I knew quite a lot of the girls since they had been students at the Sunbury Court Music Schools. They were to sing at a National Youth Festival at the Westminster Central Hall. For the occasion Brindley Boon wrote *The Kingdom* [words by Ivy Mawby] with a brass ensemble accompaniment to be provided by a group of bandsmen from Wood Green. The euphonium player was a future Chief of Staff, Caughey Gauntlett.

Getting the group together for rehearsal and providing the music copies was the responsibility of the National Youth Department. At the time, it was suggested that the singing company leaders involved should teach the song, just leaving me to bring it all together. For me, that was not an option. When dealing with a large group of singers gathered together from several smaller groups, it is crucial that they learn the song with the 'on the day' conductor; otherwise, much precious rehearsal time could easily be lost in unifying the singing of the group, leaving less time for the final touches. So we started from scratch at the first rehearsal: the Wood Green brass ensemble came to our penultimate rehearsal and then to the last one on the day. It was a very big occasion for all of us.

Immediately after the event, Colonel Bernard Adams asked me if I would be prepared to do some recordings with the group.

The youth department had dealt with all the administration and organization: fortunately they were prepared to continue doing it. The outcome was that we made several 78 RPM recordings, including some fine arrangements of Christmas songs with brass accompaniments provided by a group from the International Staff Band. The pianists involved were Marjorie Ringham, who later became the pianist for the National Songsters, and my sister Phillis Metcalf who had been my pianist with the Nelson Songster Brigade. Some of these songs have recently been included in the Heritage Series CDs now being produced and sold by SP&S Ltd.

It was interesting that over a period of time, this group increased considerably in size. Members brought along their friends and as it was not an established permanent group, there was no list of members nor were any records kept. In a letter to me recalling some of her memories, Blanche Rogers wrote:

> 'It was around 1953 that six young ladies from Barking Corps (then East London Division) would make their way regularly to rehearsals at Regent Hall under the dynamic leadership of Muriel Packham. We were not chosen: we were all eager volunteers; it felt like a great privilege to belong to the London Girl Songsters.

> 'Part of our eagerness to attend rehearsals was, of course, to enjoy a great evening of singing, albeit that Muriel did not always give us an easy time of it. Perhaps the most memorable occasion for me was when we made a recording at Maida Vale studios. During the coffee break we were gorging ourselves on chocolate biscuits when Muriel entered the room. She looked in horror at our well-earned snack and declared that it was unthinkable that we could even consider eating chocolate when we were about to sing!

> 'Our sophistication left us immediately and we were naughty, embarrassed teenagers again.

'We were all grateful to Muriel for her superb leadership and for giving us such life-enhancing experiences and lasting joys'.

It was a great privilege for me to work with Colonel Bernard Adams and the Staff Band. He was the consummate professional and treated me at all times with respect and courtesy. He was always anxious that I should be happy with the brass accompaniments. Several years later I was very pleased to be involved with him in recordings with the National Songsters and the Staff Band.

In 1951 I decided to study for a second LRAM Diploma. We were striving to save enough money to put down a deposit on a house, but I desperately needed a piano. When we moved from two rented rooms into a rented house, we felt that a piano was a 'must have'. Not only did I need it for study and for the choral work in which I was involved, but it would also provide me with the chance to teach privately, thus generating extra income to speed up the saving process. So we bought a piano on hire purchase - £10 deposit and eleven monthly payments of £10. It is still in use today. Not long afterwards, I was invited by the then Colonel F. Coutts to play the organ at his daughter Margaret's wedding. At the reception, Colonel Coutts chatted to Vic and me, and I remember the conversation almost word for word.

'How are you both getting on?'

'We're doing all right, thank you,' I replied.

'Have you got a house yet?'

'No we haven't: but we've got a piano.'

'That's right! First things first.'

In 1953, suddenly out of the blue, came an invitation for me to go to Harrow Corps to be the songster leader. Colonel Railton Howard had been the impressive songster leader there for many years. He was retiring and wanted me to take over the songster brigade. As we were still in rented accommodation, the idea seemed feasible; we were just about in the position to be able to find a deposit on a small house. All would depend on our being able to get teaching posts in the area. By that time we had been able to buy a Ford 8 car which our friend Harry Pickup had found for us. He was very knowledgeable about cars and assured us it was a good buy. Then Ted Debonnaire (deputy songster leader at Harrow), found us a very nice little house in the Yeading Lane area of Hayes. The first teaching jobs for which we applied were both within a reasonable distance of the house we wanted, the owners of which were emigrating and in a hurry to sell. Fortunately we both got the jobs, Ted secured the house, and soon we were on the move. Everything had fallen into place so we felt this was confirmation that we were doing the right thing.

It was so exciting to move into a house of our own. To us, this small, semi-detached house was a palace! It had taken us three years to save up for the deposit. We settled in, moved to Harrow Corps, where we were warmly welcomed, and in April 1953, went our separate ways to our teaching posts – Vic to Colham Manor Junior School and I to Vincent Secondary School at Northolt. I was pleased that there would be some music teaching for me – to be shared with a Mr Andrews who was head of department. So I looked forward to it, not without some trepidation – a new school is always a challenge! Northolt proved to be no exception.

* * *

*Whit Monday 1931:
Muriel carrying
Sunbeam Flag*

Parents' Silver Wedding 1940

*Sunday Morning
at Sheffield City
Training College 1940*

*Maisie Ringham with
The Wilson Sisters 1942*

61

Burnley, Nelson and Colne: Badminton League Champions 1948

Joyce Blackburn Centre of middle row

August 1950 with Vic on our Wedding day

Nelson Songsters 1948

National Youth Rally 1951
Singing Company Girls and Young Songsters
Muriel Conducting

Our street! 1930
Auntie Frances, Phillis, cousin
Eric and me.

Stopsley School Choir Singing
'I wandered lonely as a cloud

With sister Phillis and Dad (Songster Leader Nelson 1942)

National Music School at Sunbury Court 1962

Brindley Boon leads an informal 'sing song' from the piano in the lounge at Sunbury Court at the first national singing camp. Five in this group became officers, among them Major Dorothy Caddy (fifth from left), matron of Sunset Lodge, Tunbridge Wells, and (extreme right) Mrs Lieut-colonel Karen Thompson (formerly Westergaard), of International Headquarters and wife of the executive officer of the international Staff Band. Others in the picture are serving as active Salvationists in Britain, Canada, the USA, Africa and Northern Ireland.

CHAPTER SIX
'I'll go in the strength of the Lord.'
(Edward Turney)

When I initially took over Harrow Songster Brigade, Vic and I were still living in Luton. The car journeys involved were much easier than they would be today (Nov. 2003). The Salvation Army is renowned for the hospitality of its members and we experienced it in full measure at Harrow, thanks to the generosity of the Debonnaires (Ted and Doris), the Northeys (Steve and Chris) and the Honeyballs (Majors). Later, Major Cliff Honeyball became the songster sergeant. Chris Northey, who was the singing company leader, was also the accompanist for the songsters the whole time I was at Harrow. Her husband Steve was the deputy bandmaster; Captain Ray Steadman-Allen was the bandmaster at that time. They all proved to be steadfast, caring and generous friends whose later support during my husband Vic's terminal illness, his premature death, and its devastating impact on our son Andrew and me was, I believe, God-inspired.

I reported to Vincent School on the first day of Summer Term 1954. As my husband's school was in the opposite direction, I decided to cycle to school – the day of two-car families had not yet arrived. It was an easy journey, mostly along a main bus route; I quite enjoyed it, especially as there was a good bus service (along there) for the rainy days. It was to be another two and a half years before I learnt to drive a car. One Sunday when Harrow Band was away for the weekend, I was standing at the bus stop in my Salvation Army uniform in the pouring rain. The car was in the garage but I could not drive it: how ridiculous! Then and there I resolved to learn to drive. Actually, Vic taught me, which was a risky business. He was a good teacher, but I don't think I was a good pupil. One evening, having failed in my many efforts to complete a hill start, I gave up.

'How are we to get home?' he asked.

Quite clearly he was not going to drive us there; he could not be persuaded. Eventually accepting there was only one way we could reach home, I took the driving seat, started up the car and Hey Presto! we were soon going up the hill! I just scraped through the test the first time. The lady examiner, who was notorious for the many 'fails' she meted out, said to me,

'I think I'll give you the benefit of the doubt!'

Starting work at a new school is always an adventure and a challenge. I had at last been appointed to teach some music; the head teacher insisted that all members of staff spend the morning teaching English and maths to their own classes and only specialize in their own subjects in the afternoon. I never quite understood how he managed to timetable this system and even with the hindsight of many years of planning timetables, I still do not understand! Teaching English was not a problem to me, nor was teaching maths when my class was made up of some of the less able mathematicians. When later I was given an 'A' stream maths class, I really had to work hard at it. At Staines Corps we have a retired Corps Sergeant-Major, Dr. John Hebborn (Maths), a fact for which many of the young people in the corps have reason to be thankful, as he is extremely generous to the many who seek his help. How I could have made use of John Hebborn in those days!

My music teaching I shared with a Mr Andrews who was already planning to move on. He had worked with the young lady whose place I was taking. It was only later that I discovered the reason for her move out of the school; she had suffered a nervous breakdown! It was her first teaching job, and, given the circumstances, it was not surprising that she did not survive there as a music teacher. In a music lesson, the opportunities for misbehaviour are legion; in mixed classes boys are notoriously prone to make unmusical noises when asked to sing, much to the amusement of the girls but not of the teacher! Vincent School was in Northolt and had been open a mere two terms. Two single-sex secondary modern schools had been amalgamated – the pupils and staff – to form a mixed school, a recipe for disaster! Predictably problems had arisen – staff found themselves confronted by non-integrated classes of resentful boys and girls.

Some of the staff did not take kindly to the change from a small single-sex to a large mixed school. The layout of the school meant that there were long distances to be walked at change of lessons, giving further opportunity for misbehaviour. By the time I arrived at the school, things were settling down: the staff were marvellous: very talented teachers. They were also a most sociable group who really made me feel welcome from my first day there. I soon got myself involved in after-school activities; we played badminton, which was one of my favourite sports. Later they persuaded me to start a staff choir. It was amazingly good and most enjoyable – enough men for us to sing in four parts. We sang madrigals and motets as well as some modern songs and met regularly for the sheer pleasure of singing together.

My first music lesson at Vincent School is etched permanently on my memory. The music room was a lovely purpose-built detached building. Storage was good, so was the equipment. The piano was on a one-step high dais from which I always had a good view of the whole room as I played the piano. There were desks with chairs for the pupils arranged in pairs in rows. I have always needed to plan lessons, rehearsals and lectures meticulously and to keep detailed records of what has been achieved. For the first lesson on that first afternoon, I had planned the work to be done and had made sure that everything needed was ready. Little did I know that there was no chance of my plans coming to fruition. As I approached the music room from having marked my own form's register in a far distant classroom, I heard my class waiting for me – they were just milling around outside the room. My arrival made not the slightest impact on them. So I stood on the step by the door, surveyed the mob and waited. Gradually and eventually the noise subsided. I then asked them to form an orderly line, which they reluctantly and shufflingly did. The rest of the procedure can be imagined. They went into the room, slammed themselves down onto the chairs which they had moved from under the desks with the maximum of noise, and continued their conversations which had been interrupted outside. So, of course, I sent them out again and repeated the procedure, telling them to stand behind their chairs once they were in the classroom. It took me practically the whole lesson to achieve a controlled, civilized entry into the room.

They stood behind their chairs. I said,

'Good afternoon. Please sit down.'

They did: I could, now, perhaps get on with the lesson. But no! The bell rang for change of lessons and they all reacted to it by getting up and making for the door. Back they had to come and stand behind their chairs. The 'lesson' had ended and not a note of music had been heard. So, in a low, and I hope venomous voice, I said to the now silent pupils (and I remember every word),

'This should have been a music lesson; it says so on your timetable, on my timetable and on the head teacher's timetable. I know that we have not sung a note of music; you know that we have not sung a note of music, but the head teacher does NOT know that we have not sung a note of music. I will therefore now go and enlighten him.'

With that I flounced out of the classroom and off to the head teacher's room. What happened after I left I have no idea. There was no panic about missing pupils, so I presume they all sloped off to their next lesson.

My knock on the head teacher's door was answered by a cheerful,

'Come in.'

However, as I entered his room and as he looked at me, Mr Kelly was moved to say,

'Oh dear! What has happened? Please do sit down.'

He listened to what I had to tell him – the venom had not entirely left my voice – and then he said,

'I'm not at all surprised! I didn't tell you what it
was like because I thought you might not come.'

Anyone who has taught in a school, particularly a senior school,
will know that a new teacher's attitude will be assessed and
signalled round the school with the speed of lightening. (How do
they do it?) My next class was waiting for me when I returned to
the music room. On my arrival silence fell. They waited for me to
tell them to go into the room and stand behind their chairs, and
from then onwards it was all plain sailing.

Taking on the leadership of Harrow Songsters was quite a
challenge. Colonel Railton Howard was one of the foremost
songster leaders of the day. He had been an eminent conductor of
the Staff Songsters for many years and also had been in the
forefront of the development of songster brigades. His conducting
was inspiring; he had that indefinable something which brought
from the singers their best – and then more. It was an honour and
a privilege to follow him as songster leader at Harrow but also a
huge undertaking. After a strong and inspiring leader, there is
always a somewhat turbulent time (musically) before the singers
get used to the new person – some of the Harrow Songsters had
only ever known one conductor. Sometimes I have heard it said
against taking over a songster brigade, 'They are not very good'.
Well, so much the better! It is not difficult to make one's mark on
such a group, whereas taking on Harrow Songsters was a
daunting task. Colonel Railton Howard himself had singled me
out to be his successor, and, after his retirement, he gave me one
hundred per cent support. He was both very encouraging and
generous in his comments about my work – a true Christian
gentleman whom it was my privilege to know. I enjoyed being
songster leader again and had enormous support from the group.

At Vincent School, I once again had to play the piano for
hymn practices in the school hall, but I had no responsibility for
the singing, nor could I intervene. So as at Stopsley, I took my
reading book, propping it on the music stand: there was much
reading and little playing. Later, when Mr Andrews had moved
on to another school, I took on the hymn practices with his

successor, a pleasant young lady and an excellent pianist, providing the piano accompaniment. Hymn practices can be dreary, but I tried to make them as lively as possible, introducing some modern hymns which I hoped would appeal to the young people. Whole school hymn practices have almost disappeared from senior schools, which is probably just as well. Unless they are structured, controlled and the hymns are well chosen, the whole exercise can be counter-productive.

One item on my timetable surprised me: 'country dancing' (piano). That proved to be an interesting and relaxing part of my work. Two excellent physical education teachers taught country dancing for one lesson each week: I provided the music. It was such a good class and I thoroughly enjoyed playing and watching the obvious enjoyment of the pupils. Whilst at Vincent School, we nearly had a serious accident. The piano was kept on a rather high stage and it needed to be brought into the body of the hall for a forthcoming concert. We should have arranged for a piano moving firm to come and do the job, but some of the staff thought they could manage. Certainly there were some strong men available and some no less strong senior boys. I was very apprehensive but foolishly let them get on with it. The crash, as the piano fell onto the floor, was not the least bit musical! Surprisingly, not much damage was done and no one was hurt. For the concert, the music room piano was moved across into the main hall, this time by professional piano movers. We live and learn!

In a mixed senior school it can be difficult to get the boys to sing. A music teacher is very soon called on to put his/her work on show at speech days, Christmas concerts and other school events. I quickly realised that speech day was looming, and I was expected to produce some singing: I needed a choir. Fortune favoured me. In my lessons, I often left the piano and walked around the class, listening to individual voices. In one of the classes for older pupils I found a boy with a beautiful, natural baritone voice, and he liked singing. Hallelujah! Then to my delight I discovered that he was the captain of the First XI cricket team. Better still, he was a good looking young man with impeccable manners. So why not form the cricket team into a male voice choir and develop it later into a mixed choir? They were already an integrated group: the captain was a good role model and it could be quite spectacular. The captain and I discussed the matter; he thought the idea was feasible and was prepared to try to get his team-mates to co-operate. He contacted them, and back he came to me with a 'We'll do it' message. And so it was. On speech day, the cricket team, plus a few reserves who had begged to be included, gave a very hearty, yet musical performance of *The Yeoman of England*. After that there were no reluctant boy singers in the school.

Whenever I have moved from one school to another, I have always looked for an opportunity to witness as a Christian and as a Salvationist. The opportunity was not long in coming: it came in the form of the Derby sweepstake, which I think is an annual event in most schools. In a crowded Staff Room, I was included in the sweepstake procedure as the punters worked their way round the room. So a gentle refusal to participate and a clearly stated reason were sufficient to establish my Christian credentials. From that point on it was essential that I measured up to what I proclaimed. I have always found that once known as a Salvationist, questions about our beliefs and raison d'être would be asked. At this point at Vincent School the two strands of my career began to cross and re-cross as had happened at Stopsley School.

One day, when I was teaching music, a visiting group of Japanese educationalists came into my classroom. We had been apprised of the visit, so there was no surprise: I just carried on with the lesson. At the end, as they left the room, the Ealing Education Officer accompanying them came across to me and said,

'Does the name Dibden mean anything to you?'

'Yes, Commissioner Dibden of the Salvation Army.

'He's my uncle,' was the reply.

71

Many years later I met Robert Dibden of Ayr Corps who also was a relative. Robert was the pianist for me when I did a songster weekend at Kilbirnie for the then Songster Leader, Bobby Irvine. Bobby is now known throughout the Army world as a tenor soloist. He made his debut at the Scottish Music School in 1981, where this young man with the promising voice sang a solo verse of *A little ship* as it occurred in Ray Steadman-Allen's *Childhood Suite*; this was our 'big number' at that school, and that was the start of Bobby's singing career.

On another day, after a music lesson, a 13-year-old-boy stayed behind to speak to me, telling me that he played in a brass band. The following conversation took place.

'What instrument do you play?'

'The drum.'

'What type of brass band?'

'A Salvation Army band.'

'Oh, that's interesting. Which band are you in?'

'Harrow Young People's Band.'

That was a bit embarrassing: I was the songster leader, and hadn't noticed that the YP band percussionist was one of my pupils at Vincent School!

At that time I was very involved in Salvation Army music schools and with the London Girl Songsters. Once again my school work benefited from my Salvation Army connections, especially as some of the songs were suitable for school use. Joy Webb's composition *Hand me down my silver trumpet* was always popular with the younger pupils, and now that I was teaching mixed groups, I was able to use Eric Ball's *Pilgrim Song* just as it had been written. It was at Vincent School that I started the idea of lunchtime concerts, bringing in soloists such as Maureen Cooper (now Maureen Davy). When I needed a trumpeter, Brian Howard, whose parents were the commanding officers of Harrow Corps, was always willing to help.

One big occasion was a Christmas concert for parents and friends. In collaboration with the drama department, we were to stage Eric Thiman's *Flower of Bethlehem Cantata*. It is a set of songs related to, but not actually telling, the Christmas story and was to be acted out by members of the Drama Department whilst the school choir provided the singing. The last song in this cantata is, *Let trumpets sound their silver notes on high*. The piano introduction has a fanfare quality about it, but I thought I could get some real trumpeters to surprise the audience with a real fanfare. Brian was very happy to take part in this event; he also roped in two of his friends. All of them were state trumpeters. After Brian had looked at the vocal/piano score of *Let trumpets sound*, he composed a fanfare for the occasion. The trumpeters were not able to come to a rehearsal, but Brian did visit the school to see the set-up. High above, alongside the rectangular school hall was a balcony, which during the day was used as a thoroughfare – a short cut in the sprawling building. It would be an ideal place for the three trumpeters.

On the night, they had not arrived at the interval time, so somewhat anxiously I continued with the concert and watched and listened nervously for the trumpeters to appear on the balcony. We were actually part-way through the penultimate song of the drama/music presentation, when I heard a soft 'clanking' from the balcony. As I glanced upwards, I caught some movement up there and breathed a sigh of relief. The noise had been that of the spurs worn by the trumpeters who had arrived in full dress uniform of Her Majesty's Guards, complete with state trumpets with banners. The song finished; the spotlight shone on the balcony and three trumpets were raised with Guard-like precision; the most magnificent fanfare rang out. It was electric; it was magic; the whole audience was transfixed and the music teacher breathed a sigh of relief. Then the trumpets were lowered, the spotlight returned to the stage; the choir sang, 'Let trumpets sound their silver notes on high and all the earth make joyful melody'. Tumultuous applause followed the end of the concert and I looked up to the balcony to acknowledge the trumpeters. But they had departed as quietly as they had arrived.

The traffic between school and the Salvation Army was not all one-way. I got to know quite a few of this friendly staff socially. The senior master's wife was a fellow Lancastrian who hailed from Burnley – four miles from my home town of Nelson. I discovered that she was an exceptionally good elocutionist, so before long she was taking part as a guest in a Harrow Songster event. Then there was Mr Malony who had a reputation for organizing social events. Harrow Songsters had an annual Christmas supper followed by a social evening – so who better to organize the games than Eddie? When asked, he agreed to come, and he certainly lived up to his reputation.

It was at Vincent School that I was first given some additional responsibility beyond my classroom and music work. The head teacher was absent due to illness from which he did not recover. The deputy head took over the running of the school but she too succumbed to illness. This left my friend Glen Watters (Senior Master) in charge of the school: he asked me to accept responsibility for the welfare and conduct of the girls. I was very happy to do that: I knew the school well, had a good relationship with both staff and pupils, and very much admired the senior master. It was in the best interests of all concerned that the school should continue to function in a well-ordered manner and that the standards of work and conduct should not only be maintained but should continue to improve. So I, with all the rest of the staff, gave one hundred per cent support to a man who was eventually to become a college lecturer, a J P, and finally the head teacher of a large comprehensive school in Hillingdon. When he was a lecturer at Borough Road Training College, he would try to get his students into a school in Northwood where I was, by then, the head teacher: it was always a joy to see him when he came to supervise his trainee teachers.

After my son Andrew was born in February 1957, I returned to teaching. It was my decision to carry on with my career – a decision which my husband fully supported, both in word and deed. By now I had decided to try to get promotion, so I applied for a senior mistress's post at a neighbouring school. Two of us were interviewed for the job, which was given to the internal candidate who was already unofficially doing the work of senior mistress, just as I was at Vincent School. The interviewing panel asked me to apply for the next such post advertised in the Borough of Ealing. I was disappointed not to get that post, but, as has happened so often in my life, something better was waiting for me. Soon afterwards the Ruislip-Northwood Education Authority was advertising a similar post at Ruislip Manor School. I applied for it, and was appointed. At the interview I had been asked how I thought a senior post and a seven-month old baby could both be managed satisfactorily. That question would be politically incorrect in today's liberated society! However, I made it quite clear that it was my intention to continue to do a professional job; what would happen if an emergency situation were to arise was a problem which had already been addressed, and contingency plans were in place.

My mother came to live with us temporarily until I could find a nanny. Amazingly, I was asked by the then Mrs General Kitching if I needed an *Au Pair*. A Swiss Salvationist wanted to work in England prior to entering the International Training College at Denmark Hill: would I consider having her? I made no further enquiries – Marguerite was being sent to us! She came: she was lovely. Not only did she look after Andrew, she also did the bulk of the housework (unasked), including washing and ironing. 'I never had it so good!' She joined in the Salvation Army activities at Harrow Corps and (this makes me smile!) I got a baby sitter on Thursday evenings so that she could come to songster practice! She became one of the family, going on holidays and other outings with us. When the time came for her to go into the Training College, once again help was at hand! Someone at Harrow Corps told me about a lady – a trained and experienced Nanny – who now wanted a day job after years of 'living-in'. There was a good bus service from her home to ours; we arranged to meet, and the deal was done! The problem was solved. 'The Lord will provide' is a text that comes to mind!

Our small semi-detached house was in a not very salubrious part of Hayes. When Nanny Mulford arrived on her first morning, she was wearing her Norland uniform complete with hat and carrying a fairly capacious bag. From it she took her starched white apron, shook it out and donned it. She had brought with her some of the Nanny paraphernalia without which she never travelled – it included a pot of 'bump grease' which was a 'cure-all'! Every day, Andrew was wheeled out for his fresh air, pushed along a road by a fully-uniformed nanny, the like of which had never previously been seen in the vicinity. I often wondered what people thought! It was wonderful for me not having any worries about Andrew whilst I was at school. He was so well cared for! When after some twelve months, Nanny Mulford was forced to retire through ill health, we were very sad and very worried. We kept in touch and visited her until the end of her life. From that time until he was old enough to go to school, Andrew spent his days with his same-age friend, Martin Fletcher, whose mother Beryl was in the National Songsters. His father is now a soldier at Staines Corps: a small world or the Mafia Syndrome?

So, after four happy years at Vincent School, where I had made many friends, some of whom are still in contact, I moved to Ruislip Manor School where I was to work for the next eight years. There I was to have my most satisfying music teaching experience and also to have the opportunity to take on a senior role in the school's management.

* * *

CHAPTER SEVEN

'Bless, O Lord, us thy servants who minister in Thy Temple.
Grant that what we sing with our lips we may believe in our
hearts: and what we believe in our hearts we may show forth in
our lives. Through Jesus Christ our Lord. Amen.'
(The Choristers' Prayer)

From 1948 to 1960 I had been heavily involved with the
Music Schools for Girls, (i.e. Singing Company Camps) and with
the London Girl Singers. The former had featured at Salvation
Army big occasion festivals at the Royal Albert Hall and the latter
had made several recordings at the famous Maida Vale Studios.
So when the British Commissioner, Edgar Grinsted, (himself no
mean musician/pianist) suggested that a permanent such singing
group be established, Colonel Ernest Rance was given the task of
making it happen.

Much planning was needed and many decisions had to be
made. I was involved in the discussions and was invited to
become the Choral Director of the group. As I was not employed
by the Salvation Army there were many things to be considered,
not least, my family. Andrew was only three years old. The moral
and practical support of my husband would be absolutely
essential: this he gave willingly and unstintingly. The question
had to be asked and answered: 'Would it interfere with my
professional career?' By that time I was a senior mistress at the
Manor School in Ruislip. Furthermore, I was songster leader at
Harrow, a position I could only hold if I felt able to do the job
properly. A 'National' section would bring with it extra
commitments – weekends away and involvement in National
events as well as recordings. Senior Major Lena Hamlett was
chosen to be the National Headquarters Leader of the group, with
Captain Olive Feltwell as the secretary – both these ladies were
on headquarters staff. Our discussions ranged over several topics:
important decisions had to be made re personnel, programme of
engagements, repertoire and finance. Finally and after much
thought and prayer and with the agreement and full support of my
husband, I decided to 'have a go'!

The choice of accompanist (piano) was crucial. I knew exactly what was needed, having had both my sister and Chris Northey as songster pianists. Phillis had also been my accompanist at the Sunbury Court Music Schools for several years and had played the accompaniment on some 'London Girl Songsters' recordings when Marjorie Ringham was not available. Being an accompanist needs more than mere pianistic ability: it needs sensitivity to the words as well as the music, the ability to support the singing without obtruding on it and above all, it requires a rapprochement with the conductor. Both Chris and Phillis met these criteria, as did Marjorie, who was familiar with my way of working when we were involved with the London Girl Singers. So, as she lived in the London area, Marjorie was asked to take on this responsibility – I was delighted when this already very busy lady agreed. She was the singing company leader, and her husband Alf, the solo euphonium player in Hendon Band. With two young sons and, as a professional piano teacher and a much-sought-after accompanist, she was already very heavily committed. However, she found time to join me in this new enterprise and we had five happy years as members of the National Songsters.

It was decided that we would rehearse at the SP&S building in Judd Street. Our work load promised to be fairly heavy: national events, 'specialling' weekends, week night appointments and the strong possibility that we would be expected to do some recordings. Marjorie and I thought that, in view of our already busy lives and by judicious choice of members with real musical ability, we could manage with bi-weekly rehearsals. These would be on alternate Monday evenings and would have to be of an intensive nature. There would be six 'away' weekends per annum and six weeknight festivals, as well as participation in major events throughout England, Scotland, Wales and Ireland. I was optimistic that we could develop a really good choir with such a programme.

The choice of members was crucial – as a choir we would have to get quick results. With minimal rehearsal time, all members needed to be good sight-readers. However, the gathering together of the original members was not too difficult. Because of my involvement with the Music Schools and the London Girl Singers I knew so many young songsters who were good singers and musicians that we hardly had to search for members. Marjorie, of course, knew others who were unknown to me, as did Senior Major Hamlett. All prospective members would need the sanction and recommendation of their corps officer and songster leader. As ever with such groups, the Christian character of the applicants as well as their commitment to the Salvation Army had to be without question – totally non-negotiable. That many of these original members knew me and knew how I worked was a distinct advantage and it proved relatively easy to mould them into a musically homogeneous group.

The steering committee had held discussions on the subject of uniform. Was not this the opportunity for us to introduce something distinctive? Navy-blue skirts with bright red Scandinavian-style blouses were suggested, but then ruled out because it was considered that they would not be compatible with the obligatory Salvation Army bonnet. My own view was that the plainer and simpler the uniform, the better. We did not wish to be known for our uniform, but for the quality of our singing and service. So the decisions were made:15 denier black seamless stockings or tights, plain black court shoes. 'A' line navy-blue dresses were made-to-measure by SP&S Ltd. and paid for by National Headquarters. Bonnets were to be worn at all times and white gloves outdoors. 'Maculotte' navy-blue coats, again supplied by SP&S were worn when necessary and by order of the leader (i.e. Major Hamlett). There is no place for unilateral decisions in a Salvation Army music section. 'If you are in the team, you wear the team's shirt and follow the rules'.

Throughout my five years with the National Songsters, strict adherence to the accepted standard of uniform created only one problem as far as I am aware: a less-than-plain pair of shoes. Whilst we were travelling by coach to an engagement, I was the one who spotted the shoes; something had to be done about it. The young lady involved agreed that she had created a problem and that therefore she must solve it – which she did. By Saturday evening she was wearing regulation plain black court shoes. Did someone have a spare pair to lend her? Had she had time to pop out and buy a pair? I never knew: I didn't ask, but she was there in good time for the evening meeting. A teacher/leader must mean what he/she says and stick to it. The corollary of that is 'Don't say it if you can't enforce it!'

It took the National Songsters quite a while to build a good repertoire. Some of the Music School songs were suitable for immediate use and most of the songsters were already aware of the standard of singing that would be required. The basics of good singing were there right from the start: all I needed to do was to weld them into a balanced choir, to interpret the songs in such a way that I carried their musical judgement and then to inspire them to sing better than they had ever thought possible. My oft-repeated theme was, 'We must please the musicians who are listening to us – if they get the message, so will everyone else'. A recently received letter confirms that:

> 'Making the radical change from Anglican choirboy to being a Salvationist posed many challenges, not least musically. I need not have feared, for hearing the National Songsters under the musical leadership of Muriel Packham more than compensated for past musical experiences and smoothed my transition into a Salvation Army future. In particular the song 'If Thou art Near' [words by Major Mrs Ivy Mawby – music arranged by Songster Leader B.J. Boon] beautifully matching Chopin's Etude in E flat, was of tremendous help and has given life-long inspiration. Indeed the National Songsters proved to be a major influence in those early years for which I am eternally grateful'.

> *David Young*
> *Major.*

The practical side of things was very well looked after by the secretary, Captain Olive Feltwell, and later by Captain June

Kitchen who was appointed secretary when Olive was given another posting. The travelling costs to and from rehearsals and appointments were met by NHQ, as was the cost of music. Duplication of new material was taken care of in the music department at SP&S. Fortunately, one of our members, Doreen Rutt, worked there. She was invaluable in that she prepared the manuscripts of specially-composed music and duplicated the copies needed – always reliable, always on time (no computers or photocopiers in those days!). Transport was arranged, but we relied heavily on husbands, boyfriends and family to get us to the pick-up points – and meet us late Sunday night or early Monday morning on our return!

In his book *Sing the Happy Song* (published 1978), Colonel Brindley Boon wrote:

'On the front page of the first issue of *The Musician* for 1960, the British Commissioner (Commissioner Edgar Grinsted) announced that a group of thirty voices had been formed at National Headquarters under the designation of National Girl Songsters . . . the songster leader was Mrs Muriel Packham (now Mrs W. Yendell) who had succeeded Colonel Howard in charge of the brigade at Harrow and the piano accompanist was Singing Company Leader Mrs Marjorie Ringham. As some of the songsters were young wives with little children to be looked after in mother's absence, the term 'Girl' was quickly dropped from the title and National Songsters became the accepted designation.'

We made our first official appearance at Regent Hall in Oxford Street, during the British Congress in 1960, having already done a 'dress rehearsal' programme at 'Hope Town', a social services centre for women in East London. A flag was presented and handed over to Songster Evelyn Searle, (now Mrs Gordon Hughes). As I write I can see on one of my bookshelves the metal insignia from the top of that flag. When Colonel

Norman Bearcroft was clearing out the music department's rooms at National Headquarters, pending relocation, he came across this relic of the National Songsters and thoughtfully asked me if I would like to have it. So here it is, screwed into a piece of smoothed wood, which I found in the grounds of Sunbury Court – a place that has considerable significance for me. I first went there in 1948, and was thereafter involved in innumerable conferences and music schools. On my first visit in 1948 it took me the best part of a day to get there from Nelson by train and bus. Now I can drive there in three minutes to visit my family. My son, Andrew is the manager at Sunbury Court and lives there in the grounds with his family. Even more importantly, he met his wife Else-Anne at Sunbury Court when the North London Division was holding its music school. Else-Anne had come from Norway to work there for two years. Andrew was a temporary member of staff at the time: Ted Baker, the manager was short-staffed. That was an amazing coincidence – or was it more than that? For me it was miraculous, as by seeming chance my son met his future wife who is a lovely daughter-in-law, and the mother of my grand-daughter Marianne and grandson Michael.

The National Songsters' first weekend away was at Nelson (Lancashire), my home town. The songster leader was my brother-in-law, Tony Metcalf. I had readily agreed to his request for us to go for this 'ground-breaking' occasion: obviously taking this group to my home corps was a great event for me. We were given a civic welcome and much was made of the fact that I was a 'Nelsonian'. The whole weekend was a huge success: I always felt that we were very fortunate to have Major Lena Hamlett as our leader – she was brilliant! Her relationship with the members, her preparation and leading of meetings and her quiet, Christian influence on everything that happened made a tremendous impact on all of us.

We had our first 'romance' on that weekend too. Two young men from Harrow Corps were travelling on the Friday to Scotland at the start of their holiday: Gordon Hughes and John West.

'Why not stop off in Nelson?' I asked them.

This they did and attended all the meetings. After the final meeting on the Sunday evening, several of the songsters had to get to Manchester to catch the night train to London (the first of many over-night journeys to be endured!). Gordon offered Evelyn and her friend a lift to Manchester – this started a romance, which led to the first National Songster wedding. Several of us were there when Gordon and Evelyn got married at Harrow Salvation Army. It was interesting that when the birth of their first child was imminent, she nevertheless was there on the back row at a London engagement. Three weeks later, when we were having an official photograph taken, there was Evelyn again, this time in her usual place on the front row, having given birth to their son in the meantime.

Thus we embarked on what was to be a very busy period in my life, which although exciting, and sometimes exhausting, was also fulfilling. The more we sang together, the easier it became. We had an intensive rehearsal once a fortnight and usually managed to snatch some rehearsal time on weekends away. We even, on one occasion, had a rehearsal on the coach, which was crawling along behind a carnival procession. I liked to arrive at our destination in good time so that we could get ourselves organized on the platform and test out the acoustics. Good or bad, the acoustics had to be experienced so that the singers knew what to expect, especially as a large part of the ensuing programme was to be choral work.

Many were the musical talents of the members of the National Songsters – pianists, flautists, elocutionists and of course vocal soloists. Mary Edge (later Miller), who joined us when she came to London as a student, was an outstanding example of the consummate musician: an excellent pianist and an out-of-this-world singer. I have a precious recording of her singing *Mary had a baby* when we were the guests at a Northern Congress at Sheffield, held in the City Hall. We all loved Mary – she was such a beautiful person. I had originally met her at Sunbury Court Music Schools and the last time I saw her was when I was at the Scottish Music School in 1983. By then Mary had three children; she was dying of cancer. At my insistence I was driven thirty plus miles to see her in her home. Some two months later she was 'Promoted to Glory'. Her daughter, Sarah Miller, now works at territorial headquarters (THQ), London and is a presenter in the *Link Videos*.

Travelling home from Sheffield we had one of those experiences that come the way of most Salvation Army travelling groups from time to time: the coach driver lost his way but insisted that he was on the right road! So although we left Sheffield before the evening session we were not back in London until the early hours of Monday morning having done a tour of Yorkshire which included several diversions. In those pre-mobile phone days, some very anxious people had been waiting for hours at the usual dropping off points.

For me, Sheffield and coach problems are synonymous, as at a much later date, I went with Hendon Songsters to do the weekend meetings at Sheffield Citadel: usually one coach is sufficient for one weekend away, but this time it took three coaches to get us to Sheffield and back. We initially stopped at the first service station on the motorway. The coach driver had decided that his vehicle was not safe to drive – he would ring his office and demand another one. Interestingly enough, that coach stop led to an encounter and a testimony. 'Travelling' uniform was navy skirts, white blouse and navy cardigan or sweater for the ladies, and navy trousers, white shirt and navy sweater for the men. It was very simple and did not necessarily involve any extra expense. The ladies were able to 'express their personalities' by wearing a silk scarf of their own choice provided it was in recognizable SA colours – red, navy-blue and yellow plus white if desired – any combination of these colours would be acceptable.

We all went into the cafeteria whilst we were waiting for the second coach to arrive. A lone man, seated at a table, observed a group of songsters, approached them and asked who they were and where they were going. When he knew that we were Salvationists, he told his story. He had just been to the airport to say farewell to his only son who was emigrating to Australia. Naturally he was feeling upset and lonely; seeing this group of happy people had cheered him up. So he joined the group, they chatted to him and promised to pray for both him and his son. Then the second coach arrived and we went on our way. Little did we know that a third coach would soon be needed! Our journey to Sheffield was uneventful and very comfortable as we now had a splendid nearly-new coach. All was well - until Sunday morning: the coach had disappeared from outside the hall! Where could it be? How could anyone have driven it away? The police were notified – fortunately none of us had left anything in the coach – the driver contacted his firm and a third coach was dispatched. It was there for us at the end of the evening meeting, and all went well, and all was well. We were later informed that coach number two had been stolen by revelling football supporters who later abandoned it somewhere in the depth of the Yorkshire countryside.

From time to time, for various reasons, the National Songsters would lose a member and a replacement had to be found. There was always a list of applicants for membership, so Marjorie and I would arrange auditions to take place early on Monday evenings. Major Hamlett was always involved in this selection process. It was essential that new members could sight-read music well and were quick learners, as we had a large repertoire of songs with which they needed to become almost instantly familiar. I remember when Jacqui Connock (now Proctor) and Megan Jones came for audition. Jacqui told me she was an alto singer and I always felt quite pleased with myself that I had recognized her great potential as a soprano. However, fairly recently she revealed to me that the sore throat and the low-pitched voice were a deliberate ploy to have an excuse should she not pass the audition! I asked her to put into writing her version of events that evening:

> 'I entered a fairly large room in total fear and trepidation. Groups of young women were scattered around talking and laughing. No-one took any notice of me, so I sat on a chair at the back near the corner of the room. Another young woman entered and looked equally bemused and

seeing my obvious look of anxiety, asked if I was there for an audition. From that moment a friendship was formed which lasts to this day. We both watched everyone in silence, until the door opened and Muriel Packham, the leader of the National Songsters, entered.

'It is said that first impressions are lasting impressions. Muriel had the stance of a head teacher; she was there to do business and small talk was not on her agenda as she made her way to the front of the room. Immediately behind Muriel entered another lady who had a gracious and ladylike appeal. She smiled at me and my new-found friend and as she walked to the piano she stopped and spoke to members of the group. It was Marjorie Ringham, the pianist for the National Songsters and for the whole time I knew her she always displayed this graciousness and an interest in each member of the group. She had a most engaging smile – and was a gifted pianist. She was a loyal supporter of Muriel; stylish, musical and secure: the consummate pianist. As planned, I told Muriel that I had a sore throat. To my surprise she said,

"You are not allowed to have sore throats in the National Songsters".

Jacqui passed her audition and had four happy years in the National Songsters. She was quite right: there was not time for small talk at our bi-weekly rehearsal – hard work and no time-wasting had to be the order of the day if we were to achieve and maintain the highest of standards in choral music. With such a small but high profile group, physical fitness and stamina were non-negotiable requirements. So, no sore throats!

The Salvation Army's groundbreaking LP record was produced in 1961: 'An evening at the Citadel'. For the first time the National Songsters were joined by the International Staff

Band to record two four-part songs: *How great Thou Art* and *He Hideth my Soul*. A small group of bandsmen accompanied the singing in which the rest of the staff bandsmen were involved. The famous Abbey Road studios were used – I had been to previous recordings there with the London Girl Singers. On one of those occasions, Marjorie, as was her wont, went straight to the piano to test it out.

> 'This piano needs tuning!' she exclaimed somewhat imperiously.

> 'It has just been tuned, Madam: the tuner is just leaving.'

> 'Get him back!' demanded Marjorie.

They were left in no doubt of the imperative to obey. Back he came, retested the piano and agreed that it did need some retuning: the pitch had 'slipped'. From the studio manager to Marjorie, apologies; from me, heartfelt thanks.

For the LP recording there had been only one rehearsal. This was a tough assignment: many of the staff bandsmen were not used to SATB singing, nor were they used to a female conductor. As ever, I was very impressed with the professionalism of Colonel Bernard Adams and that of the players, such as Roland Cobb, Josh Wolford, Arthur Rolls and Terry Camsey who provided the accompaniment. Colonel Adams deferred to me in all matters relating to the interpretation and recording of these songs, making it as easy as possible for me, with one hundred per cent co-operation from the brass ensemble. Not so the male singers! They were at something of a disadvantage because they had no previous experience of working with me and therefore did not know what I would require of them. Nor were they used to singing in a four-part choir. Initially, I felt that I was dealing with some reluctant singers. It is an episode which I remember with great clarity, particularly the point where the men, alone, had to sing four bars in four parts: 'My God how great Thou art'! They persistently sang, 'My God! How great Thou art'. Even now, forty-one years later, I can hear myself finally saying to them,

'It might not matter to you, but it matters to me!'

That did the trick. When the recording was released, I immediately listened to that song and breathed a sigh of relief when the ugliness of the shortened word 'God' had disappeared.

Over the five years of my work with the National Songsters we visited many corps, small and large, and took part in congress-style weekend meetings in Scotland, Wales and Ireland – for this last venue we had the luxury of flying to Belfast. We relied heavily on people like Norman Bearcroft to write original music for us and also to make arrangements of other songs. The Negro spirituals *Little David, Mary's Baby* and a three-part arrangement of *My Jesus I Love Thee* to the tune *Flow gently Sweet Afton* are among my favourites. The singing of the altos on a 45 RPM recording of the last-named song has to be heard to be believed: the richness and beauty of the sound is exceptional.

Ray Steadman-Allen was another great composer who generously arranged and wrote for us. With words by Colonel Ivy Mawby, he arranged one of Grieg's songs for ladies voices: *The River*. It is as beautiful today as it was then, in the early 1960s. I used it recently at a territorial adult music school – it was new to almost all the singers, but they loved it. In 1998 this song featured in the reunion to mark the 50th anniversary of music schools for singing company members (girls) and young songsters in this territory. Although it is published by SP&S, I have yet to hear it sung by any other group.

The members of the National Songsters were multi-talented, but Marjorie and I felt that we needed an outstanding instrumental soloist to enhance our programmes. Who better than Maisie Wiggins (née Ringham)? We were all good friends and had worked together in the past. So Maisie joined us as the 'guest' whenever she could. Now we had a professional trombone soloist on the team to add considerably to the variety and quality of our programmes. Additionally, we were able to integrate successfully the trombone with the piano and voices in such items as *Songs of the Morning* by Eric Ball, specially arranged for us by the composer.

As time went by, it became increasingly clear to Marjorie and me that this talented group should be developed into a mixed-voice choir. Suitable music for ladies only was hard to come by – we needed something to challenge us and were reliant on the composers mentioned above, and others, to help us develop a suitable repertoire. In 1964, we were invited to sing at St. Martin-in-the-Field for the Worldwide Women's Day of Prayer. That year the service was to be organized by the Salvation Army: the preacher was Colonel Violet Williams and the Queen Mother was present. It was traditional at this service for the choir to sing *The King of Love My Shepherd is*. Eric Ball came to our rescue and wrote a special and beautiful arrangement of H.W. Baker's hymn to the tune *St. Columba*. Singing in the magnificent church was a wonderful experience: a solo verse sung by Maureen Cooper (now Davey) was beautiful and the words of the last verse rang out with great conviction,

> *Goodness and mercy all my life*
> *Shall surely follow me.*
> *And in God's house for evermore*
> *My dwelling place shall be.*

When we returned to our seats, the Queen mother looked directly at me and with a smile and a nod signified that she had appreciated the singing.

When we next needed something special for the Royal Albert Hall Festival we once again turned to Eric Ball. He wrote *The Magnificat* for us and came to a rehearsal to talk to us about it and why he had written it. In her letter to me, Jacqui wrote:

> 'He was a man of small stature, softly spoken with
> a gentleness and undisputed charisma. We hung on
> his every word. Even today that piece of music,
> now re-written for mixed voices, stands out in
> choral works as one of Eric Ball's masterpieces
> and is sung by the International Staff Songsters'.

The piano score had some solo passages, which needed a Marjorie Ringham. The vocal score was a challenge to the singers, unlike anything that had previously been written for a Salvation Army vocal group. Originally written in the key of B flat Major, it was lowered to the key of G Major when published for mixed voices.

In the early sixties, some excellent four-part songs were being published for songster brigades. So from time to time we were able to use such songs, singing them exactly as written except that we had Sopranos I and II and Altos I and II. Don Osgood's *Road of the Pilgrim* was just such a song – it worked beautifully and became a favourite with the singers and the listeners. These problems of repertoire would cease to exist if the group were to be developed to include tenors and basses. But the overriding and compelling reason for a change to a mixed group was the development of songster brigades. Surely a top-class choral group of mixed voices would not only be a role-model for songster brigades, but would also be an encouragement to songster leaders. Was this excellent choral group sending out the wrong message – that singing was for ladies and brass instruments was for men?

Those in authority seemed to agree with this line of reasoning. I was aware that for a mixed group a male choral director would probably be preferred, and I made it quite clear that I was prepared to accept that view. On 1st July 1963, a meeting was held to discuss these matters: present were – Major Dean Goffin (Chairman), Snr-Maj Lena Hamlett (Leader), Mrs Muriel Packham (Songster Leader), Captain June Kitchen (Secretary) and Captain Norman Bearcroft (National Bandmaster). The first three items on the minutes were:

1. The advisability of reforming the National Songsters into a mixed group by the introduction of men's voices.

It was unanimously agreed that this would be a wise move in the interests of songster brigades in the British Territory. Appreciation was expressed for the splendid standard reached by the National Songsters and the work of Songster Leader Mrs Packham.

2. Major Goffin made it clear that the new group would be under the continued leadership of Songster Leader Mrs Packham.

3. Songster Leader Mrs Marjorie Ringham be asked to continue as the accompanist.

Then, for no apparent reason, the whole thing was dropped like a hot potato! I could only assume that Major Dean Goffin had encountered some fierce opposition from some sources.

In January 1965 I had taken up the post of deputy head teacher at Northwood School. At the end of March that year, the head teacher was absent through illness: he never returned. This meant that I was promoted to acting head teacher: a time-consuming post of considerable responsibility. For the service at St. Martins-in-the-Fields I had asked for, and been given, a half-day's leave of absence. For the Royal Albert Hall Festivals I needed to be out of school all day. This was something with which I was not comfortable. I was exposing myself to possible criticism from members of staff and was not happy to be off the school premises on unofficial business. By this time I was also the songster leader at Hendon Corps – and a single parent! So, something had to go, and I decided to resign my position as songster leader of the National Songsters as soon as a replacement could be found. Thus in July 1965 ended for me what had been a most exciting period of Salvation Army music-making which I believe maintained a high standard of choral music which in due time the International Staff Songsters were to follow.

*

Excerpt from *The Musician,* November 7, 1964

Over My Shoulder
Behind-the-Scene Glimpses of the National Songsters

What a lot of glamour there must be in belonging to the National Songsters! So imagine many people. But there was little glamorous about the very damp, dark, grey morning when the National Songsters set off from their homes at about 3.30 a.m. for London Airport. Yet it was with great eagerness that we met together so early for we were to travel to Belfast for the Irish Congress.

As fifty of so people congregated in the waiting hall of the airport, I thought what a great witness this was to Christian joy and fellowship, which can permeate even the most dismal situation.

None of us will forget the beautiful picture presented to us in the aircraft as the sun gradually rose from behind the clouds. It was a massive ball of crimson fire sending out rays of light which tinted the carpet of cloud beneath us and edged the mountains of cloud around us. Dear God, how great Thou art! We really had 'taken the wings of the morning' and He was there. What a stimulus for us as we prepared to minister to the Irish people!

In Ireland we received the warmest of welcomes. Many friends had risen very early to greet us and take us home to a good breakfast.

We received another official, though nevertheless spontaneous welcome at the beginning of the Saturday evening festival in the Wellington Hall. Nine little Irish colleens said 'Welcome' to us in a short tableau and song, presenting our leaders with a small shamrock leaf each. This was a complete and very charming surprise to us.

One of the most exhilarating experiences of the week-end was the Sunday morning march of witness. We formed up into one long march, moving round the City Hall to the place where the holiness meeting was to be held. The whole city rang with the intermingled sounds of the many bands, and far from being discordant, this gave the effect of many, many church bells ringing together.

It was a thrill to see the great City Hall completely surrounded by our ranks as we marched along the circumflecting streets. I wondered if we needed to do this six more times before the walls collapsed.

We shall long remember the great gatherings in the Wellington Hall with the British Commissioner as our leader. We had the privilege of meeting Envoy Russell, O.F., from Cork, who stands for Christ completely alone in her area. This was a challenge to us as young Salvationists who have never had to face such a test of faith.

After a week-end of fellowship and service together we boarded the airplane watched by many Salvationists who had made the journey to the airport so late in the evening to say farewell. Around midnight we landed in London, a little delayed and rather exhausted.

Any glamour? Well, there's no doubt that the week-end had been very, very worth while.

Christine Lee

* * *

CHAPTER EIGHT
'Let all the world in every corner sing!'
(George Herbert)

The Manor School at Ruislip was quite different from any other school in which I had taught, although in one respect, with the exception of Toddington, exactly the same: the school already had a music teacher, a young Welshman who was an exceptionally good baritone singer.

The Ruislip-Northwood Education Authority was very forward-looking and was developing sixth forms in all its secondary modern schools. Many of the pupils already stayed on at school beyond the statutory leaving age in order to take 'O' level exams. Thus with other schools in that area, we were making a nonsense of the Eleven Plus examination, as many of the pupils at the top of a secondary modern school eventually did better at the age of 16 years than some of their contemporaries in the grammar schools. (At the Manor School, as hitherto, I inherited the timetable of the person I was replacing.) The Local Education Authority, in liaison with employers in the area, had developed a Ruislip-Northwood School Leaving Certificate which was a recognized worthwhile qualification for those who left school at the age of 15 years.

All this was new to me and very much welcomed. I soon became involved in the local school-leavers' exams, teaching both English and maths. The chance to get a qualification in these subjects was eagerly seized by the pupils. The only exception was a group of boys who did not like academic work and grew progressively unable to cope with it. I was given the job of getting them to work – it was a challenge! I must admit that initially and occasionally I felt like sending a very troublesome boy to a senior member of the staff for chastisement – that is, until I remembered that I was a senior member of staff myself and had to work out my own salvation! I later learned that this group of boys had brought a younger member of staff to the verge of a nervous breakdown and that some of the staff – friends of a teacher who had applied for my job – were keenly watching for my downfall!

They were disappointed – the boys gradually started to work and some of them even did well in the school-leavers' exam.

My own form was a parallel class of girls who intended leaving school as soon as possible. I coached them for the school-leavers' exam in both English and maths. Girls were expected to do well in English – better than the boys – but to struggle with the maths syllabus. However, by sheer hard work, by making use of every minute available on the timetable and with some help from the head of maths, they maintained their superiority in English and did marginally better then the boys in maths. Had those girls been at school when the school-leaving age was raised to sixteen, they would have achieved some reasonable grades in the GCE exams.

After two terms, during which I had gained valuable experience in the general working of the school, the music master achieved his ambition to get a place in the Welsh National Opera. I was asked to take on the music timetable, from the beginning of the next school year. From my point of view, there was one big problem: the 'O' level classes had one music lesson a week and the rest had two. This 4-form entry school was organised on a 'streaming-by-ability' basis. The top streams were 'too busy' with 'O' level work to have more than one music lesson per week. I was not happy with this inequality as psychologically it downgraded music as a school subject. Before she had worked out the timetable ready for the autumn term, I put my case to the Head teacher (Miss R. M. Allen) who was a very forward-looking lady. She had sympathy with my point-of-view: either one or two music lessons a week for all the classes. She promised to consider the matter, and when the new timetable came out, to my great pleasure she had given each class two music lessons per week. This started a period of my music-teaching life which was most fulfilling and rewarding.

At school, for the first time ever, I had 16–18 year old boys to teach. With two music lessons a week from the first to the sixth form I had a wonderful opportunity to develop music skills. My lessons had three components: music reading, music appreciation and singing. Obviously these three facets of music-making overlapped. As ever, I had to plan carefully and record meticulously what had been and what was to be achieved in each music lesson – that was the only way I could work.

As I write (2003) there seems to be a revival of SATB singing in senior schools. At the Manor School, in the late 1950s and early 1960s, I had no difficulty in getting adolescent boys to sing. Lots of really good three-part songs were being published – some were arrangements of popular and folk songs and some good original compositions. My classroom strategy with the 14–15 year-old-boys was simple: the third stave of the voice parts was the 'baritone' line – often it was just the alto written on the bass clef. By this point in their musical education, the boys were able to read that third stave. As I wandered round the classroom listening to individuals, I would spot a 'grunter' and quietly say to him,

'I think you could join the baritones now.'

He knew his way to the back corner of the room where his pals were. From then on he was reminded to obey my baritones' rule: 'Sing what you can, mime what you can't.'

One young man – John Bull (a name I could hardly forget) – was singing an octave lower than his fellow baritones. I quietly asked him to stay behind after the lesson. He was a tall young man, and I pointed out that his voice was in his boots, a very long way down. So I suggested that he should bend down, take hold of his voice, and put it into his head. As I write this, it sounds quite ridiculous. From the look he gave me, so it did to John. For me, it was a spur-of-the moment thing: but it worked! He thought it was a miracle and so did I. Now he really was a baritone, whereas he had been a basso-profundo.

I was able to develop a four-part choir – SATB. We sang madrigals, motets and modern four-part songs. Every Friday morning they sang in the school assembly and they participated in school concerts. At Christmas, the school had a carol service at the Ruislip Parish Church in which the choir participated. I had planned to conclude the service with a recording of the *Hallelujah Chorus* from *The Messiah*. When the choir heard about this, they were somewhat indignant!

'Why can't we sing it?' was the cry.

I pointed out the difficulties, but they were adamant – they wanted to have a go. So we did – and they did it – setting a precedent for all future carol services. I had to apologize to them for underestimating their abilities.

The local Ruislip-Northwood Music Festival provided an opportunity for us to compete against other school choirs but more importantly to have an independent assessment of our work by an adjudicator. It became an annual event in the calendar. There was always great jubilation when we unfailingly beat into second place the local grammar schools in the 'School Choir (secondary)' class. I was so fortunate to have all the students for two lessons a week: it was the happiest and most rewarding time of my music-teaching career.

During the Christmas season 1956, I had seen, whilst still at Vincent School, a television performance of Menotti's short opera *Amahl and the Night Visitors*. We did not own a TV set, but a good neighbour across the road invited me to her house to watch it. I was spellbound; it was so beautiful. Later I bought a copy of the full score and realized that it was not so difficult as it had sounded on the television. The non-negotiable requirements were, a) – a top class pianist, b) – a female singer with a big range of notes, and c) – a boy with the voice of an angel and the looks of a mischievous rascal. I determined to produce it at school when those three essentials were covered. A flautist was needed but as there was a good recorder band at the Manor School, I knew there would be no problem with flute parts. I was prepared to wait until I felt we had the personnel in the school choir to embark on this enterprise. I did not have long to wait!

My involvement with Salvation Army choral music continued apace. National Music Schools were a regular feature of the school summer holidays. Each year the standard of singing was better than the last: I was always on the lookout for new, challenging vocal music. Sometimes suitable songs were written specially for us, as when Eric Ball produced an anthem-type setting of *Sing we the King* [words: C. Silvester Horne]. In 1969 I found two songs set to music by Kenneth Downie: *The Cleansing Power,* [words E.A. Hoffman] and *Completely Thine* [words: L. Taylor-Hunt]. They were just what we needed. The name of the composer meant nothing to me; I needed to know.

'Who is Kenneth Downie?'

'He's a young bandmaster in Southport.'

'Does he know we are singing two of his songs?'

'I shouldn't think so.'

'Could we let him know?'

So he was contacted. As a result, at the end of the final festival, a young man was seen purposefully walking down the centre aisle at the Fairfield Hall. It was Kenneth Downie. He came straight to me and was overjoyed to have heard his songs.

Recently he told me,

> 'It proved to be an inspiring experience. I was taken aback by the quality of the performances and the musical sophistication from such a young group of musicians.'

A few weeks later, the same girls sang *The Cleansing Power* in the Royal Albert Hall at the General's Farewell. People used to say 'How can you get such a high standard in just a week?' Part of the answer was the daily learning/rehearsal routine: probably the equivalent of about eighteen songster practices. Most importantly, there were no absentees: everyone was present at every rehearsal. Are there any songster leaders who could say that about their rehearsals? I think not!

A start had been made on divisional music schools in 1953 at Grendon Hall, Northamptonshire, and I had been asked to organize and direct the music there. Major G.B. Smith, who had been on the staff at the very first 'Singing Company Camp' at Sunbury Court in 1948, was the divisional commander. My pianist for that week was the talented and charming Mrs Colonel Bernard Adams, wife of Colonel Bernard Adams with whom I had worked on recordings with the London Girl Songsters.

I continued at Harrow as Songster Leader and was kept very busy. We did the usual special events and 'specialling' at other corps, with the normal number of hair-raising experiences. The one I remember most was when the songsters went by bus to a Saturday night festival somewhere in the East End of London, - it was literally a hair-raising near miss! The driver must have thought he was driving a single-decker as he damaged part of the roof of his double-decker bus by going under a low bridge. We thanked God that no-one was hurt and that we were able to continue our journey and fulfil our obligations. I am sure that all Salvation Army music groups have similar or more horrific stories to tell of travels to engagements.

During this time Major Dean Goffin arrived on the music scene in Great Britain; I was soon to get to know him because of my involvement with music schools, choral workshops and leaders' residential weekends at Sunbury Court. Our first meeting was at Harrow Salvation Army. Soon after his arrival in England, I invited him to Harrow to conduct a songster practice. It was obvious to me from the start that here was a musician of no mean stature. He was very impressive. It was a special occasion for Harrow Songsters and I'm sure that almost all of them enjoyed it. My reservation concerned the basses. Dean told them that they 'sounded like bulls'. I admitted to myself that I had occasionally had the same thought, but prudence prevented me from articulating it – after all, I had to live with them! Still they took it in good part, and psychologist that he was, Dean found a way of giving the basses some genuine praise later in the rehearsal. The renowned Harry Kniveton – well known throughout the Salvation Army as a beautiful baritone soloist – was a Harrow Songster at that time and I felt privileged to have him in the group and grateful for his unfailing support.

One of my favourite songs for songster brigades is the setting by Eric Ball of *Psalm 8.* I decided to use it at one of those big occasions – the opening of the refurbished hall at Harrow. It includes a lovely quiet passage in four parts for the men: 'And the Son of Man that Thou visitest him'. A mere four bars, but we worked at it to make it beautiful: it was beautiful in the rehearsal, but on the day it was shatteringly unbeautiful. My knee jerk reaction was to put my head in my hands and say, 'Oh! No!' That was dreadful I know, but I had had a shock. Anyway, it was momentary and we carried on. There was a *Da Capo* sign at the end: the same four bars were coming again. I said a prayer and gave the men a beseeching look – and they sang it as rehearsed – magic!

Still at the Manor School, I made my first acquaintance with the PUNISHMENT BOOK. Until then I did not even know that such a thing existed. The circumstances of the discovery were rather unusual. The school was over-subscribed, in part due to the growing fifth and sixth forms. Later on a new school had to be built. In the meantime, temporary accommodation was to be used for the first years in a building some three-quarters of a mile away from the main school. An experienced lady teacher was drafted there to take responsibility for the boys and girls. Other specialist teachers went there for certain lessons, but it was not a satisfactory state of affairs, and the lady teacher was not able to cope with what was quite a difficult situation. She was brought back into the main school and the deputy head and I were temporarily drafted in to run this annexe. I wasn't very happy about it because it took me away from my responsibilities as senior mistress and also interfered with my music. In addition I had to teach other subjects there. Teachers from the 'big school' came and went but I was stuck there for almost half the week.

During this time the school had a 'full inspection', dreaded by all members of staff. I was particularly annoyed, as I was not following my usual timetable; would they come to see me give a geography lesson or a maths lesson? Anyway, they arrived when I was just starting a religious education lesson. Then a most opportune thing happened. Police came to investigate the loss of a bicycle. The HMI was left with the class as I dealt with the police. Wonderful! I have to admit that I made no effort to hurry the police along and when I got back to the classroom I found that the HMI had done the necessary and kept the class occupied. So I told him I would give him a good report! That was the end of that. Unfortunately I didn't get a chance to let any inspectors hear some good singing.

Before he left, the HMI asked to see the PUNISHMENT BOOK which I found in a drawer. Any punishments had to be recorded in it, giving date, day, time, offence, punishment meted out and finally signed by the administrator of the punishment. It made very interesting reading, and I was appalled at the frequency with which the cane had been used. So, I'm afraid, was the HMI. All the dates in the book were before Mr Hill and I had been drafted in to sort out the mess. However, one entry in the book was quite priceless - the HMI laughed with me! The elderly lady who had resorted to the cane so often had reported that two named boys had each received two strokes of the cane. In the 'reason' column was written, 'Urinating at competitive levels'.

It is so important for the teacher to act in such a way that the pupils feel they are treated fairly. My 'firm, fair, fun' slogan should be adopted by all people in authority over others. Children in particular will not forgive unfairness. In most situations of conflict in a school, there are three possible outcomes: a win/lose situation, a lose/win situation and a win/win situation (a lose/lose situation was not on my agenda). The teacher must strive never to get himself into a lose/win situation. Nor should he subject the student to that situation. The win/win result of a conflict is the most desirable. I see no problem with saying to a teenager 'If I do . . . will you do . . . ?' or the other way round. I have proved over and over again that this way of resolving conflict is the least damaging to relationships and leaves no resentments.

When the new school year started, I went back into the main school. Not only had being at the annexe interrupted my own class work and my choir practices but it had also created some problems which were waiting for me when I got back there.

Being a senior mistress meant that sometimes pupils were sent to me to be disciplined. It was not an easy situation with which to deal. One had to be seen to support the staff whilst at the same time occasionally having a sneaking sympathy with the perpetrator of the crime. The teenage girls were often a problem for the young male teachers. I remember the time at Bradley School in Nelson when we had teachers on 'emergency training' – a short course for demobbed men. They were all somewhat older than the normal trainee teachers and they did not find teaching rather attractive girls who were 'early maturers' at all easy. One of these 'trainees' begged the head teacher not to give him the fourth year girls to teach! (14 and 15 year olds).

On one occasion at the Manor School a very attractive and somewhat mature girl was sent to me 'to be caned'. In my position, I was always prepared to look into a problem but I was not prepared to be told what punishment (if any) was to be meted out! The story that unfolded was this: Mr L. had asked her to take a note to another member of staff – a useful ploy to get a 'nuisance' out of the classroom. As she strolled out of the room, the teacher foolishly said,

'Don't hurry, will you?'

Acting on his suggestion, she eventually arrived back in the classroom some twenty minutes later. Mr L. displayed his annoyance by asking her what took her so long.

'You told me not to hurry, so I didn't,' was the
pert reply.

As Mr L. considered this was insolence, some form of punishment was required. Matters came to a head when the girl refused the punishment, which was to run three times round the perimeter of a play area overlooked by several classrooms. At that point she was sent to me for 'the cane'. She admitted to me her transgressions but was not prepared to run round the playground in full view of her contemporaries. Some compromise had to be reached – I believed in the need to negotiate. It was late in the year and twilight would come soon: she agreed to do the run after school when no one would see her. There was no question of any further punishment, although I thought Mr L. deserved some for creating such a situation. I discussed this with him when I told him of the outcome, giving him some advice against using sarcasm on teenage girls and pointing out that if he did need to send a student to me for punishment, he was in no position to prescribe what that punishment should be. There is a saying: 'Sarcasm is the lowest form of wit'. Certainly it is a fact that teenagers hate to have it used on them. One morning, a lovely 15-year-old girl came running into my empty classroom – she was quite 'beside herself'. Her teacher had been sarcastic to her. Amid tears she said,

> 'My dad was sarcastic with me before I came to school; now HE'S (Mr S) been sarcastic, and he's NOT EVEN MARRIED!'

Music was more than ever a big part of my life and my Salvation Army work – Harrow Songsters, music schools, YP leaders' weekend conferences, recordings and writing series of articles on 'Songstership' for the then *Bandsman and Songster* weekly paper – was running smoothly as was my home life. I was really enjoying school work: not only the music, but also the experience of being a senior member of staff.

In 1962 my husband was diagnosed as having cancer and on March 13th 1963 he was 'Promoted to Glory' at the age of forty years. My life and that of my son, Andrew, was shattered. The staff at the school were marvellous, especially the head teacher and a young teacher, Dorothy Youell, who from 1963 right to the present day has, with her husband Geoff, been a tower of strength, as the following illustrates:

In early March 1963 the country was in the grip of a very cold spell. One Saturday morning I discovered that all the water pipes in my home were frozen up. Whatever could I do? A phone call brought Dorothy and Geoff to my rescue. They arrived at the house wrapped up against the bitterly cold weather, and had brought a kit of tools.

'Leave us – we'll be in the garage.'

They refused offers of food and hot drink.

'We've brought it with us.'

And so the morning passed. I was very busy indoors – Vic was terminally ill. Then came a knock on the door: the workers had finished.

'No need to worry: we've lagged all the pipes.'

Occasionally in the past I had thought it would be nice to do part-time teaching but now I knew that having a full-time permanent teaching post was probably going to be the salvation of this little family of two!

* * *

CHAPTER NINE

'Music produces a kind of pleasure
which human nature cannot do without'.
(Confucius)

In June 1963, out of the blue, I received a telephone call from Major Timbrel, the commanding officer of Hendon Corps. Could I help out with the songsters? It was holiday time: no one with any experience of being a songster leader was available. My friend Marjorie had found it to be too heavy a commitment. Like me she had a home and a family to keep going, she worked professionally as a piano teacher and was pianist for the National Songsters. In the Salvation Army she was much in demand as an accompanist – vocal and instrumental – and was also involved with her sister-in-law, Maisie Wiggins, in her recordings and 'specialling' both in the United Kingdom and overseas.

Major Timbrel was soon to go on holiday herself. My first reaction to her request was an unequivocal 'NO'. Life was not easy, my son was my number one priority and moving from Harrow to Hendon could prove to be disruptive for him. The time and the travelling involved might be a problem – I already had enough and did not want anymore! But Major Timbrel did not give up easily – she was very persistent and persuasive. I finally agreed to go to Hendon to 'hold the fort' until she returned from furlough. Twenty-one years later I was still there.

In that day and age it was not unusual for songster practices to continue throughout the summer holidays. People generally went away during the school holidays but at Hendon we managed to keep rehearsals going through the summer. Songsters were coming and going, but the commitment to being part of the Sunday meetings at the corps was still there: the songster brigade was never on holiday! In any case we could not afford to go for some six weeks without rehearsals, as one of Hendon Songsters' special events was September Song, a programme of choral music with guest soloists. Either my deputy or I worked on those songs during what we used to call the 'silly season', then two good rehearsals in September would be sufficient to get them up to standard for this special event. All the time I was at Hendon I kept a record of songs rehearsed and the dates when they were sung in public. Keeping records was always essential for me – otherwise things would get in a terrible muddle.

When the commanding officer came back from her holiday, the problem had not disappeared. Would I carry on a bit longer? I was quite enjoying working with a songster brigade again and despite the work-load involved, felt unable to refuse to continue. I capitulated: I would stay 'for the time being' to give her a chance to find a songster leader. For me, it was decision time: my open-ended commitment to the songster brigade forced me to reconsider Andrew's position, and I decided to take him to Hendon with me. He soon became a YP band recruit and eventually a member. Hendon Corps, then as now, was blessed with a group of potentially top-class musicians - amongst them the 'Cobb boys' and the 'Ringham boys'. Andrew was in good company. Now it was no longer necessary for me to hurry back to Harrow after the morning meeting: Andrew had been staying with my friends Steve and Chris Northey until I arrived back from Hendon. We were able to accept some of the invitations to meals that we received at Hendon. When this happened, Sunday really did become a 'day of rest'. However, there was a price to pay: the many little tasks that I had been in the habit of doing on Sunday afternoon were still there waiting for me when we arrived home after the evening meeting.

About this time Andrew was enrolled at the Harrow Saturday morning music school run by the local education authority. One Saturday he came home and said,

'My cornet teacher knows you.'

'What is his name?' I asked.

'Mr Mitchell.'

His wife Veronica, was a member of the National Songsters, and strangely enough, Alex Mitchell's parents had been stationed at my home corps in Nelson; I remembered him and his sister Catherine. Perhaps it wasn't strange though, because, wherever we Salvationists go, to whatever parts of the world, we always seem to meet someone whom we have met at some other time, in some other place. After a round-the-world holiday in 1997, I was relating my experiences to a group of former colleagues: I had been with Salvationists in Cape Town, Perth, Sydney, Brisbane, Wellington and Los Angeles. One of the group said,

'It's not the Salvation Army, it's the MAFIA!'

The 'time-being' for which I was staying at Hendon stretched with the elasticity of a rubber band. I began to feel as if I belonged there. To my surprise, some many months after my pro-tem move, it was announced in a meeting that I had now been transferred to Hendon Corps. John Cobb, sitting in the trombone section of the band, said in a stage whisper,

'We couldn't afford the transfer fee until now'.

It was not until 1984 that I finally retired as songster leader at Hendon: my retirement weekend must rank as the strangest such event in the annals of the Salvation Army – I wasn't even there!

Having a responsible and interesting job proved to be my salvation from Easter 1963 onwards. Whilst at school I was fully absorbed in my work. Unexpectedly, the move to Hendon Corps proved to be therapeutic, although I have to acknowledge that in the social context of a corps, being a forty-one year old widow was not an easy situation. People were very kind to me but loneliness in a crowd and in a familiar setting is more difficult to bear than loneliness in a solitary situation. I was determined to do whatever it took to help my son recover from losing his father (as much as it is ever possible to do so). Hendon seemed to be the best place for this to happen.

During this difficult time I got tremendous support from the National Songsters. I had not been able to go with them on their last 'specialling' weekend in March 1963: Marjorie stood in for me. In a service at Harrow Corps in memory of Vic, I was surprised and absolutely overwhelmed to find the National Songsters taking part – it was very moving. The next scheduled weekend away was not easy, and I found conducting some significant songs almost too much to bear, especially Eric Ball's setting of *In the Secret of Thy Presence*. Tears were never far away. After that, I gradually got back to near normal and by the summer time I was well able to take control of whatever we were singing. A significant occurrence actually helped to restore my emotional and spiritual strength when Major Dean Goffin invited me to conduct the massed songsters at the Royal Albert Hall Councils Festival. It was both a challenge and an honour for me. On Major Goffin's part it was an act of compassion.

At school I was getting a great deal of experience in management and much pleasure in teaching music which was the only subject on my timetable. Choir practices had to be held at lunchtimes once a week and one day a week before morning school: barely enough rehearsal time but they were quick learners. However, popular though they were with the pupils, my rehearsals were less so with some members of staff. One lady who taught many of the older boys and girls in the choir, entering them for English language, English literature and history GCEs, objected vociferously: the choir rehearsal time would be better spent in doing some revision. My belief is that group singing in a controlled situation involves the whole person – it is a mental, physical, emotional and spiritual experience.

> 'Whenever people are making music together, at
> that time they are better human beings'.
> Yehudi Menuhin.

I was not convinced that choir practices were a waste of time.

> 'If my pupils don't do well in their GCE exams,
> I'll scratch your eyes out!' were her final words on
> the subject.

When I had told Vic of this confrontation and the scratching out of eyes, his question was,

> 'What, both of them?'

At the first convenient opportunity and as pleasantly as I could, I related this snippet of conversation to the lady. She was gracious enough to see the humour but not enough to withdraw her opposition. It was in this sort of situation that I had learnt the value of compromise. I needed to show some flexibility. So, after Easter the GCE pupils were not to come to choir practices until they had finished their exams. They were indignant but I insisted, without telling them what had prompted the decision. From Easter onwards, these students would come to the door of the music room and ask,

> 'Why can't we come in? We aren't doing any other work.'

I kept them out, although I privately thought it was nonsense. Once exams were over, all those staying on for the sixth form were back in the choir. One boy, who had been named as likely to get poor results, as he spent so much time with the choir, did exceptionally well. HALLELUJAH! He had been a shy introvert, but I believe that singing had given him confidence because he had a very good natural bass voice and this confidence had spilled over into his academic work. The ability to negotiate with both pupils and staff proved later to be a valuable asset. There are times when a bit of give and take is called for. In some situations however, where a principle is at stake, one has to abide by the words of St Paul,

> 'And having done all, to stand' (Ephesians 4:13).

In my previous teaching posts I was used to having visits from music advisers. At Stopsley School the Bedfordshire Adviser had come to see me. His main concern seemed to be that a stock of percussion instruments in the music room cupboard were not being used - he wanted to know why. My reason was that I was not convinced of their value in the situation where singing, music theory, music reading and music appreciation were being taught. He was, however, very anxious that the equipment should be used. At that point I admitted to not having a clue what to do with it and suggested that he could help me by arranging to come and do a demonstration lesson. He was much less enthusiastic about that and said he would first come to see me teach. At a later date, this is what he did - and that was the end of that! I did not see him again! A Mr Slack was music adviser for Middlesex when I was at Vincent School. He was very supportive. The Japanese educationalists' visit to my music room had been arranged by him: he came to Harrow Salvation Army to preside over a songster programme on one occasion.

The Ruislip/Northwood Education Authority at that time had no music adviser but the Manor School did have a visit from Mr Frith (Her Majesty's Music Inspector for the southern region). After spending a lesson with me, he asked to hear the school choir - tantamount to a Royal Command! He arranged to pay another visit to make a tape recording of some of the choir's repertoire,

> 'When I run courses for music teachers they tell
> me that senior boys will not sing. If I tell them that
> I have heard a secondary modern school choir
> singing unaccompanied Madrigals and Motets as
> well as modern SATB vocal music they will not
> believe me. I just want to be able to present them
> with the evidence.'

All through my teaching career I have tried to provide opportunities for making and listening to music outside the classroom situation. I felt it important that students should listen to live music. Hearing and enjoying good music is a soul-uplifting experience, and, having the opportunity to sing together to a good standard is a valuable part of music education. Thus it was that I applied for my choir to take part in the annual 'Ernest Read Christmas Concerts' at the Royal Albert Hall. We became part of a huge secondary schools' choir, accompanied by an orchestra and with Ernest Read as conductor. It was a wonderful experience for these young singers and their obvious enjoyment was very gratifying for their teacher. Then there were the annual visits to Guildford Cathedral arranged by Mr Cox – the recorder teacher who also taught religious education and started every lesson with a prayer: he was greatly respected for that. He arranged for both the recorder ensemble and the school choir to spend a day out listening to and making music.

1. Coach to Hazelmere to a recorder workshop presented by the famous Dolmetsch family.

2. Coach to a primary school to give a short concert. (The head teacher was a friend of Mr Cox.)

3. We all had a 'school dinner' which was remarkably good.

4. Off to Guildford to the cathedral to present a recital.

I know that singing in a cathedral is a very special, never-to-be-forgotten experience. My pupils did not really believe that, in spite of my telling them. Ron, a senior boy, started a conversation with me as we travelled to Guildford,

'Why are we going to Guildford Cathedral? Have we been invited?'

'Mr Cox has asked us to go with the recorder ensemble and take part in the programme. They go every year!'

'Will there be a lot of people there?'

'I don't know. It depends how many people are visiting the cathedral.'

'If there are only a few people listening to us, why are we going?'

'Just for the privilege of singing in a cathedral.'

He shrugged and turned away, totally unconvinced!

When we arrived, the pupils were thrilled to see a large notice advertising a recital by 'The Manor School Choir and Recorder Ensemble'. A good crowd had gathered and we presented our recital. It was obvious that the listeners were enjoying our music, that they were really listening, not just hearing. A good performer can always tell the difference! Ron came to me at the end of the recital:

'Now I know what you mean!'

That visit to Guildford Cathedral became an annual event, as did participation in the Ernest Read concerts.

This forward-looking Education Authority also encouraged music in schools by arranging for groups of musicians to come into schools to give recitals. Occasionally, a cinema in Harrow would be booked for a schools' concert performed by professional musicians. The programme was given to us well in advance so that time could be spent on the works to be performed, thus enabling the pupils to understand the music to which they were listening. Within the school context, it was important that pupils were not taken out of school except with the goodwill of the staff who would normally have been teaching them. Most teachers were co-operative: some even enjoyed the free time created by a class's absence at a recital. A few were not prepared to release pupils to listen to music when they were working on an examination subject. This was an absolutely valid stance and was respected. As senior mistress and head of music, I was able to organize all these events with very little disruption to the school timetable and I tried to ensure that all pupils, at some time or another, heard live music. One memorable evening a group of sixth-formers went to a Promenade Concert at the Royal Albert Hall. Tchaikovsky's Sixth Symphony was on the programme: we had been studying it at school using the full score. I had a seat in the stalls, they were promenading. It was a great moment when they spotted me and waved their scores at me. I think I watched them more than the orchestra as they read their way through the symphony.

There is no doubt that at that time Ruislip-Northwood Authority was in the forefront of the development of secondary schools. Secondary modern schools were encouraged to develop GCE examinations and to make provision for those who wanted to stay on into the sixth form to do 'A' level subjects and exams. Officially, all pupils at the Manor School were 'failures': they had failed to pass the 11+ exam. Yet, with dedicated teaching and our faith in them, they got good exam results at fifth and sixth form levels, often faring better than many of their contemporaries who had 'passed' the 11+ exam. We were the forerunners of the comprehensive school. Another local innovation was that schools could offer specialist courses from the third form onwards – so much for the notion that today's specialist schools are new! At the Manor School we developed a three-year art course. Each September we would receive a small number of pupils onto this course, whilst transferring out some pupils to other schools with different specialisms.

One September two boys joined us on the art course. Naturally they came to me for music, and as was my wont, I walked around the classroom whilst a familiar song was being sung and listened to the new boys. No problem! They both had musical baritone-type voices and were singing easily with none of the shyness that usually inhibits adolescent boys. I mentally earmarked them for the choir but waited for an opportune moment to invite them to join, stressing my need for two extra tenors! To my delight, they immediately accepted the invitation. Then I discovered that they both played the guitar: I auditioned them and liked what I heard, and also what I saw! They were bright with lots of personality. It was not long before they were playing in school concerts and entertaining the whole school in the Christmas festivities: they were a smash hit! Tony Munroe and Ronnie Wood became permanent features at school concerts, and Ron went on to become a guitarist of 'The Rolling Stones'. Since then – the early sixties – I have had only one contact with him. Having read in the national press that he had married the mother of his children, I somehow got his mother's address: she said she would pass on my letter. So I wrote to him and received back a very friendly reply. He has since developed his art, and when in San Francisco a few years ago, I passed an art gallery which was displaying his work. I went in and asked if Ron was in town. No! he would be there the following weekend. We were due to leave the next day, so a message was left,

> 'Tell him his old music teacher at Manor School
> was asking after him'.

The gallery owner looked very surprised when I said that Ron had been a tenor in my four-part choir,

'You're kiddin', was his response.

My grandson, Michael, has a painting that Ron did for me at school: I had seen and liked some of his work. When asked if he would do something for me, he agreed but said that he would need to come to my home to see where I would want to hang his picture. My immediate reaction was one of surprise and some reluctance, followed by the inner voice that said, 'Come on! Trust him!' So we went home, surveyed the empty spaces on the walls, made a decision on positioning and finally he measured the space to decide on the size of the final article. The picture – an abstract – was finished, and he came home with me to hang it. I paid him £5, which was quite a lot of money in those days. Its value as a piece of Rolling Stones memorabilia must have increased somewhat since the early sixties.

It was in 1963 that, thinking of my ambition to produce the opera *Amahl and the Night Visitors,* I decided that the two absolute essentials – a girl with the soprano voice that could soar, and a boy with a voice like an angel – were available. Elizabeth Nelson, a fifth form girl, would be able to sing the female lead, and Terry Donavan, a thirteen-year old who had a wonderful treble voice which he tried to hide (he did not particularly like singing) would make an ideal Amahl. Elizabeth had done quite a bit of solo singing and when entered for the local musical festival, had always won first prize in the girls' solo section. Amongst the senior boys there were plenty of candidates for the Kings' roles; indeed, at the end, we had a full cast, plus a full cast of understudies. In the opera Amahl plays the flute. Terry couldn't do this, but we had some excellent recorder players who could manage the flute part, one of whom was chosen to sit under the grand piano, play the music whilst Terry mimed it. The other essential was a top-class pianist: who better than my friend Marjorie Ringham? She agreed to join us for the final rehearsals and the three consecutive performances just before Christmas.

This production developed into a whole school effort. The art department designed the set: the technical studies people made the set and whatever props were needed. Costumes were designed

114

and made by the needlework department. Lighting was the province of the science department whilst the physical education staff choreographed the dancing of the shepherds. Although I was overall responsible for the production, including the music, the head of English took on the job of producer, a role with which he was quite familiar. Much of the work could be done in the classroom and integrated into the syllabus. All rehearsals were as and when possible, without impinging on normal school work, particularly where pupils were studying intensely for their examinations.

A full rehearsal for a day in the autumn half-term holiday was scheduled. Everybody was there except 'Amahl'. I rang his home – he was 'playing out' said his mother. I explained what we were doing at school and that it was vital for him to get to school immediately.

'He told me he was doing something in a play,'
she said.

'Doing something! He has a star role!'

We did not have long to wait for him to appear. Last year I went to a reunion for a Manor School year group. When the organizer knew that I was going to be there, she contacted Terry Donavan, and although not in that year group, he came to see me. He is now a robust fifty-something year-old man. He talked about 'Amahl', and how it had awakened his interest in singing.

'You were a tyrant' he said, 'but you made me do
it and I've come tonight to thank you.' He has
been singing as a semi-professional ever since.

We did a full dress rehearsal performance for the whole school - it all came together, with Marjorie at the piano, and the recorder player under it. The curtains went back and revealed the inside of an impoverished cottage with Amahl's mother sweeping the floor with a broom. The first beautiful notes rang out: 'Amahl! Amahl! Time to go to bed!' From then on the opera tells the story of the three Kings seeking shelter in the cottage as they follow the star to Bethlehem.

For three evenings the school hall was packed. A few friends from the Hendon Salvation Army came, as a result of which it was suggested that we should take the production to Hendon SA for the second half of a Christmas music evening promoted by the band. We needed no persuading! All those involved in the play were thrilled to be invited to go to the Hendon Corps and I know that the people in the audience that evening not only enjoyed it, but were moved by it. Fairly recently, at a conference at Sunbury Court, Steve Cobb said that, as a boy, he had been in the audience that night, and the opera had made a profound impression on him. By this time in my school-teaching career, I had realized that for the students, achievement in out-of-school activities is almost as important as the academic work. They are not mutually exclusive. Indeed, I believe that good performance in the arts, in sport and in music and drama as extra-curricular activities has a direct influence on the quality of effort and achievement in the classroom. Every young person should be given the opportunity to try out a whole range of activities, not only to discover in what they can excel, but also what is not exactly their 'cup of tea'!

In the following summer term, the deputy headship of nearby Northwood School became vacant. I had not been thinking of moving, but nevertheless I was interested in promotion both professionally and, as a single parent, from the finance point of view. Several friends urged me to apply for the post. Somewhat half-heartedly I decided to have a go. Application forms were available from the education offices, but such was my lack of enthusiasm that I didn't see any point in filling in a form when they already had my details on file. So a short letter to the director of education at the Uxbridge office, telling him, a) that I would like to apply for the post, and b) that he had my details, was all that I felt was needed. The letter was posted and then forgotten. We were well into the autumn term before I was called to the education office for an interview. The head teacher of Northwood had not contacted me to offer a visit to the school. Either he wasn't interested in my application or he thought it best for me not to visit the school: people do sometimes withdraw their applications after such a visit. He did however ring the Manor

School on the morning of the interview to offer me a lift to the education office – an offer which I declined with thanks: I had my own transport! I remember nothing at all about that interview except being called back into the room to be offered the post. Visiting Northwood School before the end of the autumn term, I was given details of the timetable I would be inheriting from my predecessor: English country dancing with mixed classes would be a challenge! Northwood School had a good reputation and I was pleased to be moving into what I thought was probably going to be the last school of my teaching career – and so it proved, but not quite as I expected. It was not without some sadness that I left Manor School – I had enjoyed my time there. As head of music, I had experienced the most satisfying period of music teaching in my career. But I was moving on.

* * *

CHAPTER TEN

'God moves in a mysterious way His wonders to perform'.
(William Cowper)

In 1965 Northwood School was a four-form entry secondary modern school but it was as far from the tarnished image of a 'secondary modern school' as it could possibly be. Academic work of a high standard was already a feature; there was a small but growing sixth form and both staff and pupils seemed to be well motivated. Although the school-leaving age was officially fifteen, the majority of pupils stayed on to take examinations in the fifth year. In a *Northwood School Diamond Jubilee Magazine* (1935 – 1994) a retired Head of English, David Hood, whom I had appointed in 1971, wrote:

'My first impression of the school was an all-pervading atmosphere of friendliness, happiness and contented bustle. I immediately felt welcomed and 'at home', and this feeling stayed with me for the next eighteen years. The head was then Mrs Muriel Yendell, her deputies being Jim Edwards and Miss Lynan, and between them they ran the school highly successfully and with little apparent fuss'.

For there to be 'little apparent fuss' good organization was necessary and, as I soon learnt, it was essential for all members of staff to feel that they were part of the communication chain. Steps were taken to ensure that this was so. There were however, some aspects of the school that did not appeal to me: rigid streaming meant that some pupils were not expected to do well in examinations: 'O' levels were out of their reach. There was still the local Ruislip/Northwood school leavers' certificate, with which I had been involved at the Manor School, but, as long as the school-leaving age remained at fifteen, a small percentage of pupils would always miss out on national examinations. A very good commerce course was available, but only to girls, and there was nothing of equal worth available for the boys.

Sports-wise, it was a rugby school – they were rather proud of that! The summer game was cricket for the boys, with tennis available for everybody and netball for the girls, who played hockey in the winter. English country dancing also featured in the curriculum; my predecessor was a country dance specialist and the school was renowned for its prowess in inter-school competitions. Taking up a senior post at a new school is somewhat daunting – all eyes were on the new deputy head and I was alert for the inevitable 'try-out'. This came from some of the female staff on my second day. I was summoned to the ladies staff room to go and intervene in what promised to be a nasty confrontational situation. Having sent back a message that they surely did not need me to sort out their problems, I heard no more: that was the end of that!

Hymn practices were once again on my timetable: half the school at a time in the main hall. It was a bit daunting – this meant that once a week, in two sessions, I came in contact with every pupil in the school. The staff also came and sat at the sides of the hall – this was lesson observance with a vengeance! Actually, I was very nervous but had learnt not to show it, having experience of the big occasions in my Salvation Army work. Never have hymn practices been prepared more meticulously! Never had there been a more judicious choice of hymns! Once the standard of behaviour, including effort, had been established, all was well – except for two boys at the back of the hall who 'tried it on'! I had learnt early in my career that the very first incident of unacceptable behaviour must be dealt with; let it go and a more serious problem is created. This *modus operandi* I emphasized to all young teachers and students with whom I worked, and also preached at conferences for singing company leaders and songster leaders at Sunbury Court. In this instance at Northwood School, I remember that I walked purposefully to the back of the hall, and quietly dealt with the miscreants – I can't remember what I said, but it had the desired effect – they chose to join in with the still-continuing singing, and that was that. It made life easier. I think the first lesson for all teachers and choir-directors is a golden rule,

'Start from silence'.

This rule applies however long you have to wait for the silence you require. There are some useful comments about this in a very good book published in 2002: *How to be a successful choir director* by John Bertalot (published by Kevin Mayhew Ltd.). What applies to the choir, applies in the classroom! I became involved at Northwood with probationary teachers and students on teaching practice from various colleges and I had the opportunity to pass on to them this lesson learnt the hard way.

My next big problem was of a very different nature. The school secretary was a formidable lady who had been in charge of the office for many years, and was a devotee of the head teacher, Mr J. The latter's various interests meant that he was often off the premises, sometimes unofficially. As a Welsh rugby fanatic, he would leave school early if that was the only way he could get to the match. I got the impression, that when that happened, the School Secretary Mrs F was in charge. This assumption proved to be correct one Friday afternoon, when, because of some serious misdemeanour – (serious usually meant harming or putting at risk of harm some other pupil) I decided to send a girl home mid-afternoon. Obviously, parents had to be contacted and a letter to be taken home would be required. When I gave a draft letter to Mrs F for typing, she pointed out to me that I could not do this. Mr J was the only person who took such decisions; the matter would have to wait until Monday. The fact that Mr J was on his way to Ireland for the Wales/Ireland Rugby match which was to be held on the following day, only strengthened my resolve to deal with the problem there and then. The discussion went along the expected lines, - Mr J was absent, the deputy was officially and legally in charge and the matter was serious. In the end, the letter was reluctantly typed, the parents contacted and the girl went home.

On the Monday morning I made an appointment to see the head teacher (Wales had been defeated by Ireland, so he was not a happy man). I told him what had happened, although I rather think he already knew.

'I am not comfortable with the situation!' I said.

'Well, that is the way it is; I make all the decisions.'

'If you cannot agree to my dealing with something, which, in my opinion, will not wait until your return, I find myself in a very difficult position.'

'That is what has always happened and that is the way it will be,' replied the head teacher.

'In that case, I suggest you re-advertise for a Deputy Head, as I am not prepared to accept your dictum.'

If he was surprised, he did not show it; after a moment's consideration he said,

'There is no need for that! If it occurs again, your judgement about the proper course of action will prevail.'

It did not happen again. That was the Easter term and by the end of March, Mr James, who had been limping rather badly, was away from school on sick leave, never to return. He died in June that year (1965), some time after I had visited him in hospital in Reading. The funeral was to be in Uxbridge, and the Director of Education rang to ask for the school choir to sing at the funeral service. There was no school choir!

'Well I'll get another school to do it!'

Of course that would not do! So I said that we would have a choir by the appropriate date. An appeal by me to the fifth and sixth-formers brought more than enough volunteers and we worked hard whenever we could get together, both before, after and during school hours, doing a crash course in SATB singing. They met the challenge and were proud to sing in the church as a tribute to their head teacher.

I soon discovered that there is a huge difference between being a deputy head and actually being in charge of a school. The phrase 'the buck stops here' comes to mind. From that point on, everything that happened in the school was my responsibility. That term as deputy head stood me in good stead; I already knew the school and the staff. There was however, much to learn. I moved into the head teacher's room; some of my teaching had to be written out of the timetable. Country dancing was the first to go although I still retained some classroom work and continued to do so for the next fifteen years. Now that I was 'acting head teacher', a young member of staff, Mr L, a top-class science teacher, came to see me about registers. (Five out of six of his secondary modern schools' sixth form physics students had achieved 'A' grades in their A level physics exams: the sixth had a 'B' grade.) There was a calculation to be done each week and he was now querying the need for it. Teachers are notoriously unhappy about anything to do with registers.

'Why must it be done?'

'I'm afraid I don't know,' I replied.

'Well, I think it is a waste of my time and I'm not going to do it!'

He was very pleasant, very polite and very firm. I immediately decided that I would look into the matter and told him so.

'In the meantime I want you to carry on doing the calculations and I'll let you know the outcome as soon as possible.'

He did and I did. Mr Cryer, who had responsibility for the registers, had no idea why the exercise had to be done:

'We've always done it.'

'What do you need it for?' I asked.

'I don't think we use it at all!'

So he told the staff that they need no longer do the Friday percentages, but not before I had been to see Mr L to give him the good news personally!

That same term a summer afternoon school concert had been scheduled; I was anxious to see and hear what was to be presented but was not happy with what I heard. So as tactfully as possible, I suggested a few changes – some of the prepared work would not be ready in time. A good friend of mine would probably be willing to bring her son to play some trumpet solos, which she would accompany at the piano. So it was that the Salvation Army, in the person of Marjorie and Paul Ringham, came to Northwood School in my first summer there, and it was the start of a relationship that lasted throughout my time at Northwood. At a later date I became involved in an interesting BBC project; I was asked to provide music for the hymns to be sung in the Friday morning 'Daily Worship for Schools'. A mixed choir of schoolchildren and adults was formed, to be accompanied by a Salvation Army Band, to record twelve hymns. So a group of bandsmen from Hendon accompanied hymns sung by some Hendon Songsters and Northwood Senior Pupils. The recording was made at Golders Green Theatre. It was a good learning experience for the Northwood students – we were all amazed that the recording had to be halted whenever a London Underground train passed beneath the building!

We were also involved in a Television recording; I was asked to provide a choir of eight boys and eight girls aged 13 – 14 years. Obviously this would be a good experience for the participants – we were to be the backing choir for Max Bygraves singing *Any dream will do* from *Joseph and his Technicolour Dream Coat* [A. Lloyd Webber]. What fun! Choosing just sixteen, plus two reserves was not easy: preparing the song was! The producer sent one of his music people to the school to check up on us! He went away a happy man. The recording was on a Sunday at the TV studios in Shepperton. A double-decker bus was sent for us; parents were welcome and, best of all for the students – they were to be paid. I had agreed that they should each receive £20 of the £40 standard fee. The other £20 went into the school funds. We actually created a 'Max Bygraves Fund': when cash was needed for something that could not legitimately be taken from any other source, I would say to the secretary,

'Take it out of the Max Bygraves Fund'.

In those days £20 was quite a lot of money for a young teenager; they had enjoyed a lovely day out, been given lunch and innumerable drinks and snacks, and, best of all, a Max Bygraves autograph. He chatted to them throughout the day; they sang well, and later, their final excitement was seeing themselves on television. From time to time the school received small amounts of money when the recordings were used again – 'royalties'. In this way the 'Max Bygraves Fund' was kept solvent for a very long time.

I soon was able to go on a course for head teachers re. administration and management. Actually, a lot of what I learnt was common sense, which is not particularly common. There was, however one very important formula that I latched on to and it stood me in good stead throughout the whole of my stay at Northwood School. Drawing up a timetable for a mixed secondary school is a most daunting task – the bigger the school, the more difficult the job. In consultation with the senior staff, and particularly heads of departments, it is the head teacher's responsibility to allocate the amount of time to be spent on each subject and also to decide which members of staff should teach which groups. Some teachers preferred younger pupils, others enjoyed sixth form work. The formula I learnt so early on in my career as head teacher enabled me to check easily and quickly that each year group was being given a fair allocation of teacher time in all subjects. Without such a check there was a danger that some of the younger age group would suffer for the benefit of the examination years.

I had previously compiled a timetable at Stopsley School where the head teacher had offered the experience to anyone interested. Miss Millam had done all the preliminary work when she gave me the 'jigsaw' to complete. With a picture jigsaw, the last few pieces are usually easy to put into place: not so with a school timetable. It is often necessary to undo some of the work in order to make changes that will facilitate completion. At Northwood, I took the first opportunity to do the timetable myself: it seemed the best way to familiarize myself with the working of the school, but most importantly, with all the individual members of staff. Northwood was a mixed school with a big fifth year, and a small, but growing sixth form. This timetable would be somewhat complicated. Once all the decisions had been made and the analysis completed, I took the work home and finished it there: progress would have been very slow had I tried to do it at school, as having the necessary long stretches of uninterrupted time was just simply not a possibility. I fairly soon decided that as the school grew bigger and more staff were appointed, a teacher who had the skills and experience to draw up a timetable for a large mixed school would be needed.

In 1965, when I was catapulted into being in charge of Northwood School, the Ruislip/Northwood Education Authority ceased to exist: we became part of the London Borough of Hillingdon. This new borough council announced its intention to abolish the 11+ examination and to change to the 'comprehensive' system of education; an early decision would be made about the future of each secondary school. In the meantime, no head teacher posts would be advertised, which meant that I would continue as acting head teacher for the time being. I made up my mind to forget that in another year or two I might revert to being deputy head and just to get on with the job. The school was running well, academic standards were high and I made it my business to see that these were maintained.

The punishment book gave me cause for concern, as it had done at the Manor School Annexe – caning seemed to have been an acceptable form of punishment. I questioned Mr Cryer – from senior master he had been promoted to deputy head (acting) – and other senior staff. My first big decision at Northwood was to ban the use of the cane – and any form of corporal punishment – by anyone except the deputy head, and then only in the most exceptional circumstances. I knew that some staff thought this would have an adverse effect on the general discipline in the school but I was convinced it was the right thing to do. By not banning the cane outright, I made a concession to those who feared the worst and privately resolved to ensure that there were enough positive influences in the school to make the cane totally redundant. At a much later date, three senior boys were sent to me for smoking on the school premises – they knew it was unacceptable. Even now I can visualize the scene in the head teacher's room. I was seated at my desk and these three big lads were standing in a row 'on the carpet'. After some questioning on my part and some feeble answers on theirs, I said to them,

'Come to the office at the end of afternoon school.
There will be a letter for you to take home to your
parents. Tomorrow, I shall require an answer,
either by letter or in person.'

They appeared to be dumb-struck. They looked at each other in consternation and then one of them said,

'Couldn't you just cane us?'

As I write, I can hear myself saying,

'No, I'm not going to cane you!'

It was not easy to keep a straight face!

In my first year in charge of the school I made no big changes. The aim was to maintain and improve the academic standards and to ensure that pupils of all abilities were given the opportunity to achieve the best of which they were capable. I was gaining experience of managing a school of some 600+ pupils. Although the statutory leaving age was 15 years, the number of pupils staying on to do GCE and later CSE gradually rose to 82%, and more and more were coming back for the sixth form. My responsibilities were legion: pupils, parents, staff – both teaching and ancillary – cleanliness and safety of the building and site. I was responsible to the authority for everything that happened on the school premises. The buck stopped at my desk. Meanwhile the education authority was debating its proposed change to comprehensive schools. When the decision had been made, all vacant headships would be advertised in the national press, and the acting head teachers would be invited to apply. Peter Hill, my friend at the Manor School with whom I had worked for several years, was in the same boat as I. Our schools were chosen to be developed into six-form comprehensives, and we both applied for the headships. It was a nerve-racking time; we had been in charge of our schools for some eighteen months and would find reverting to deputy head somewhat difficult.

Peter had his interview a week before mine; when some outsider was appointed, he was devastated! He was a man with a good degree, was an excellent teacher and administrator. (He soon left the school and took up an advisory post in the borough where my friend Doug Collin was to work.) Then my turn came. If Mr Hill with a degree, good experience as a deputy head and acting head had not been appointed as head, what chance did I have as a mere female with no degree? My music qualifications gave me the obligatory 'letters behind my name', but I did not think that would count for much. The Staff sent me 'Good Luck' messages on the fateful day. As I went through the education office, a senior officer said 'Go for it', and I did. There were five other candidates – all men – but my big advantage was that I had actually experienced running the school for nearly two years. No one ever knows all the answers but my time as acting head teacher probably meant that I knew more answers than the other interviewees. I went back to school, no longer the acting head teacher – I was now the real thing! The news had preceded me and arriving back in school, I was congratulated and presented with a huge bouquet of flowers – very exciting! At the fairly recent speech day, the chairman of the education authority had said, much to the amusement of the staff, that the school would soon have a PROPER head teacher: this had hit the headlines in the local press. Well, now I was a proper head teacher!

Plans were afoot for the enlargement of the school into a six-form entry comprehensive: at least a 50% increase in the number of pupils over the next five years and a corresponding increase in the sixth form. Extensive new accommodation would be required and I was involved in all the discussions and planning. There would be an equivalent increase in staff numbers – both teaching and ancillary. The eventual size of the school would warrant a second deputy head. Mr Cryer, the acting deputy head, reached his retirement age as did his wife, the head of the English department. They were given a lovely party – both had been at the school for many years. The new deputy head was Mr D.J. Edwards, who came to be referred to as simply DJ – there was another Mr Edwards on the Staff – DA. Both were Welshmen. We were soon to be joined by a second deputy head who was also Welsh. I sometimes thought I was in a foreign land!

DJ had a reputation for having good relationships with both pupils and staff, and so it proved. He taught maths, but his hobby was 'outdoor pursuits'. The borough had an 'Outward Bound' type of centre in Snowdonia; regular weekend and holiday visits to this facility became a feature of the extra-curricula programme. The school raised the money for a first minibus, soon to be followed by a second. There was never any shortage of volunteers – both staff and pupils – to go to the mountain centre. I always wanted to experience for myself ('just checking') such aspects of the school's activities, so one weekend my husband and I went with a group (by car – there was no room in the mini-bus) into the Welsh mountains. I was very happy with what I saw and experienced that weekend. DJ had all the necessary qualifications and experience for such school journeys. The conditions at the base and the firm control of all expeditions and activities were exemplary.

For a second deputy head I was looking for someone who could offer an academic subject up to 'A' level, who had proven management skills and who would be able to take responsibility for the huge time-tabling 'jig-saw'. A friend of mine with whom I had worked at the Manor School applied for the post, and was subsequently short-listed. Her subject was biological sciences. After I had moved from the Manor, she had become deputy head there, with responsibility for the timetable. As head teacher I was on the appointing committee, but at the interview was not expected to join in the general conversation, unless directly questioned by the Chairman. I was, however, invited to question each candidate at some point in the proceedings. Finally, the panel whittled the choice down from six to two, and my friend, Dorothy was one of the two. At that point I felt obliged to reveal my friendship with her, and that having worked with her for several years, my expressed wish was that I should take no further part in the proceedings – but I kept my fingers crossed. She won the day, and joined us at Northwood at the beginning of the next term. This second deputy proved to be worth her weight in gold: a brilliant teacher respected by both staff and pupils and a timetabling wizard!

The Senior Mistress (Miss Lynan) was another staunch member of the management team: I was so fortunate to have the unqualified support of these talented and entirely dependable colleagues. She was a needlework specialist, which she taught to 'O' and 'A' level standard. I was surprised to discover that the 'A' level needlework syllabus included the study of social conditions in the U.K. On one occasion I took a group of 'A' level needlework students to participate in the 'soup run' operated by the Salvation Army's Regent Hall Centre. It certainly was an education not only for the students but also for the head teacher. When Miss Lynan retired early for medical reasons, an internal candidate was appointed senior master: a Mr A. Kelly who was another staunch, dependable member of staff, whose 'O' and 'A' level geography groups always got good results, and whose interest in outdoor activities supported DJ in outward-bound pursuits. This team of senior members of staff put all their energies into the colossal amount of planning and hard work that went into changing a four-form entry secondary modern school into a six-form entry comprehensive. They were all still there when I retired in 1980. Through many trials and tribulations – overcrowding, lack of space, continuous presence of workmen involved in building extensions, problems with senior staff at the education office, threats of strikes from the National Association of Schoolmasters' members – the school continued to flourish and eventually we all celebrated the opening of the large extensions: another era in the school's history had begun.

* * *

Manor School 1964
'Amahl and the Night Visitors'

Hendon Y.P. Band 1968

Eric Ball conducting
Stainer's 'Crucifixion'.

Hendon Songster Local
Officers with Major Mingay

Hendon Songsters with Major and Mrs D Ward 1982

The National Songsters with Captain June Kitchen and Major L Hamlett 1962

The First National Songster Wedding. Page 83

Northwood School Head boy (Tom Stowart) with the girl prefects 1967

Northwood School. The kidney machine thermometer

National Songsters' reunion 1975

My last day at Northwood School 1980

General Coutts with 3 boys who had each achieved 9 'O' Levels

Hendon Songsters' Timbrel group 1980

Hendon Singing Company recording for the 'Jimmy Young Show' Christmas 1967

CHAPTER ELEVEN

'It is the best of all trades, to make songs
and the second best to sing them'.
(Hilaire Belloc)

When in 1963 I went to Hendon to look after the songsters, I could not have imagined that I would still be there in 1984. On two occasions I relinquished the position of songster leader. Although I love directing choral music, I have always found the position to be onerous and time-consuming – a big responsibility with a commitment to provide suitable choral music for Sunday worship. We were kept busy with special events, weekends away, and participation in divisional and national events. The spiritual and social needs of both the group and each individual were also the responsibility of the songster leader. For this, a good set of 'local officers' is essential; the choice of songster sergeant is critical and crucial. Over the years I was fortunate in having such people as Mrs Joan Cobb, Lieut-Colonel Joy Steadman-Allen, Colonel Netta Jakeway, Jocelyn Noble-Grestry and Hazel Renshaw in that position. Indeed, I was always well served with hard-working and loyal local officers. I shall never forget the colossal workload of Eddie and Chrystal Fisk who were the music librarians: they created a 'no problems' situation.

Thus, after I had become responsible for running a large secondary school, I told our Commanding Officer, Major Pegg, that I would be happy to relinquish the job if he could find someone else to do it. He took me at my word and the next week he had found someone; 'It must be a person he knows, is available and is very good!' was my thought. And so it proved. It was Colonel Ray Steadman-Allen, no less! He lived fairly close to Hendon Corps and at that time was not involved with any other corps music group. I was able to leave the songsters – not 'in the lurch' but in the capable hands of one of the Army's 'greats'.

'Now', I thought, 'I can have a complete break from Salvation Army responsibility at Hendon Corps!' This was not to be.

Not long after the change of leadership, Margaret Saunders, the singing company leader, was involved in a road accident when a lorry ran onto the pavement where she was pushing her baby in his pram. Peter, her son, was unscathed, but Margaret was seriously injured. When asked if I would look after the singing company for the time being, there could only be one answer: 'Yes'. It was the first time I'd actually been responsible for a singing company, although at the Sunbury music camps I had gained a lot of experience with 11–18 year-old girls and at school I was used to teaching this age group in mixed classes. I found it most enjoyable: they were a good lot of young people. The only problem I had was one that I believe is experienced by most singing company leaders – the wide age range. Where else in the education system does one have to teach an age range of eight to sixteen in one group? Jeanette Bosanko, well known in the UK and in the USA for her outstanding choral work, told me that in rehearsal she favoured splitting the choir into three smaller groups according to age, and sending them off with teachers to learn the song before bringing them back together to work with her as a whole choir. Ann Fuller (Staines Corps), who is a qualified and very experienced music teacher, taught her Clydebank Singing Company as a whole group. She felt that the younger ones, who might find the work difficult, would benefit by being with the senior members: it would only be a matter of time before these eight/nine year olds became the older ones on whom new members relied. Both methods are valid; at Hendon I kept to what Margaret had done, and the whole group rehearsed together.

Quite a number of them were in the eight to eleven age group: many of these were blessed with good voices. Coming events cast their shadows before as Roger Cobb and Sandra Youngs did some solo singing and later sang together. In the fullness of time, Sandra became Mrs Roger Cobb and I used them as duettists with Hendon Songsters. Keith Morley, now a Salvation Army officer, was another good singer, as were the three Thornton children, and the Cobb girls – I don't believe there were any 'passengers'. They soon got used to a new leader – or so it seemed. I remember in great detail the second Sunday that I conducted them. They sang in a half-hearted way – it really was a poor show. I could not let that pass, so at the end of the meeting they were told to stay on the platform. I then asked them to sing the song again, this time in the way they had been taught – they were in no doubt about my displeasure. People in the hall were mostly standing in groups chatting: others were on their way out. As the children sang, the noise from the body of the hall gradually subsided, and silence fell. I was aware, as most conductors would have been, that the singing had really captured the attention of the listeners, and that the singers were actually communicating with them. The moral for the children was that there is only one way for a choir to sing: with voice, intellect and heart. It was a lesson well learnt that did not need to be repeated.

We sang every Sunday morning in the meeting at Hendon and took part in some events outside the corps. Two of these were unusual and outstanding. A weekend 'specialling' at Bedford Congress Hall was a challenge that became an achievement. The singing company had a group of 'local officers' who took away from me all responsibility except for the singing. Any 'specialling' weekend requires a lot of planning and preparation – it all happened. At the time, Bedford Congress Hall was a glorious hall with a high ceiling – beautiful for singing! The young people really rose to the occasion. The other exciting event was when we were invited to take part in the Jimmy Young Christmas Day broadcast. That really was very special – but we only saw Jimmy Young as we were walking away from Broadcasting House! I have a tape-recording of the broadcast: JY introduced us as realistically as if he had actually been there listening to us. Roger Cobb and Sandra Youngs were the solo voices for *Good King Wenceslas* and his 'page', and Keith Morley also featured as a soloist.

Eventually Margaret was fit to resume leadership of the singing company. For me it had been a really enjoyable experience; it was a privilege to be the Hendon Singing Company Leader – albeit temporarily. Now I would be able to concentrate on my work at Northwood School which was more time-consuming than anyone could imagine. But it wasn't to be.

Eventually Colonel Ray Steadman-Allen had to move away; I was asked to take on the songsters again. I knew it would mean a lot of hard work and a huge personal expenditure of time and energy. The group had increased in size and was much in demand for 'specialling' and territorial events. However, pressure was applied to me from several benign sources and eventually I agreed to have another go. Being the Hendon songster leader was always most enjoyable – they were such a good group of people to lead. They wanted to learn and expected to be well taught. A Salvation Army group of musicians be it band or songsters, youth chorus or YP section, has a responsibility to perform (for want of a better word) to the highest standard of which it is capable. My dad used to say to me, 'Good enough is not good enough. Only the best will do.' Service and dedication are the cornerstones of Salvation Army music-making. In 1945 I had accepted that, and was not prepared to renege on my allegiance to God and the Salvation Army. In any case, to be a Hendon songster leader again was a tremendous privilege. Somehow or other I would juggle the demands of school, home and the songsters. However, after a few more years as songster leader, knowing that Paul Ruby would very much like to take on the songsters, and being aware that he was more than competent, I suggested to the corps officer that he should be given the opportunity. He was very happy to take over and it was not until 1978 when he was moved across to being the bandmaster, that I once again took on the songsters for what proved to be the last time.

In that year, I had decided to keep a day-by-day diary. Reading it recently, I concluded that it could have been any year – my already hectic timetable soon became somewhat overloaded. Northwood School plus Hendon Songsters proved to be a very challenging programme. The following extracts from my diary of 1978 make interesting reading:

Monday 20th March: - At school all day. The liaison committee met at 4 pm. Back to school in the evening for a concert for parents and friends.

The liaison committee was a group that met after school to discuss individual pupils who were giving us cause for concern. Staff involved were the form teacher, head of school (lower, middle or upper) the 'special needs' teacher, the authority's welfare officer and, if need be, the psychologist. Having been briefed about the pupils concerned, they all came ready to discuss the problems and to prepare a plan of action. Either I or one of the two deputies would chair the meeting. As ever, an agenda was published, minutes were taken and notes made of the agreed proposed actions. Procedures were in place to ensure that all relevant staff was kept informed.

Wednesday 12th April: - To Belmont School for lunch, then afternoon meeting with director of education. Evening reception at school for American students and their leader, Jim Shea (whom I had met on my USA Exchange visit), Mayor and Mayoress present.

Exchange visit to Long Island, USA: - We had been given an opportunity to get involved in an 'exchange' programme, and thought it would be a good thing for the school. I decided to make the initial visit myself. It was a wonderful three weeks; some time was spent at the senior high school, but my base was Gelinas Junior High on Long Island. What amazed me and made me somewhat envious was the amount of space! Classrooms were big, sports facilities were huge, the school concert hall was like a medium-sized theatre, the dining room was a capacious restaurant and the spacious gymnasium housed several badminton courts. A library as large as the average public library was the 'icing on the cake'.

My weekends were free; the first I spent with Brian Nutty and family in Toronto and the second with Philip Smith and family in New York. The 'Mafia' syndrome came into play. After a Saturday evening band festival in Toronto, a young man came to speak to me: it was John West who had been in my songster brigade at Harrow. A second young man, visiting from Australia, approached me!

'Do you remember me? I used to deliver your meat when you lived in Luton!'

Incredible: it was David Novell who had moved to Australia with his Salvation Army officer parents and had once been a Saturday morning delivery boy for my butcher - Songster Leader Hubert Janes.

Wednesday 25th April: - Very late home from heads of department meeting. 7 pm back to school for governors' meeting.

Heads of department meetings were very important; all senior members of staff would normally be present. My policy of ensuring that all teaching staff had an awareness of what was happening in the school, and what was going to happen in the future, meant that agendas and minutes were available to everybody. A governors' meeting was held once a term: the agenda was based on my written report submitted to the chief education officer some weeks beforehand. A senior education officer would be present, and the head teacher was there to be questioned by the governors.

Thursday 13th May: – pm to Hayes Stadium for the Hillingdon School Sports (Secondary). After tea, back to school for 'open door'. Had two parents to see. Home at 9.30 pm.

The 'open door' was just that! One evening a week the head teacher's room was open for parents from 7 pm, to 9 pm or later if need be. (Thursdays when I was available, changed to Wednesdays during my Hendon Songster Leader years.) The two deputies each did one week in four and I was there on alternate weeks. Parents were welcome to come with or without an appointment: they were all aware of this facility and were reminded of it from time to time. Sometimes parents rang to say they would be at the 'open door' - this meant that we could have the pupil's file ready, get an up-to-date report, and invite the form tutor to come to meet the parent. In all the years that this system was in operation, every teacher invited to be present readily agreed to be there. Why did we do this? It had become obvious to me that some parents could or would not come to parents' consultation meetings. Those who could not, welcomed the opportunity to see a senior member of staff; those who would not, were personally invited to 'open door'. Rarely was this invitation refused. Very occasionally it was arranged for a specific subject teacher to be present. We had a large 'open door' book in which details of the meetings were recorded, including proposed actions, leaving room to record the eventual outcome. Occasionally members of staff would ask if they could sit in on an 'open door' consultation and a senior member of staff would even want to be on duty officially. One head of department expressed doubts about this facility. 'Nobody came', was his complaint. I thought that was a cause for rejoicing! Another member of staff, (head of middle school) having had a parent to see him, left me a note on my desk:

'Mrs Yendell,

Good Morning!
Only one customer - my patch.
3rd year options.
You have looked a bit down lately. Here's an extract from your large Bible:
'When the righteous are in authority, the people rejoice'.
I for one notice we have a happy staff.
Have an interesting day in authority.

John Levermore'.

Tuesday 11th July: – Busy day, then my first songster practice – very enjoyable. A songster locals' meeting followed. Everyone worked hard.

Sunday 16th July: – Three meetings. My first Sunday as songster leader. First song – bad start. All right after that.

Monday 11th September: – Managed to get the governors' report done and sent off to the education office. Corps council meeting at 7.45 pm. Home at 10.45 pm.

A whole week in September from my diary.

Monday 25th: – Not a good day at school: felt very weary. On 'bus stop' duty. Songster finance committee meeting. Home at 10.30 pm.

'Bus stop' duty meant supervision of the crowds of pupils waiting for a bus at Northwood Hills. We had received complaints about behaviour, and this supervision, undertaken voluntarily by the staff, was the answer. As head teacher I felt quite strongly that I should take my turn.

Tuesday 26th: – A better day at school. Back in the evening for first year 'commendation awards'.

Commendation awards were given for any commendable work, be it in academic subjects, practical work or physical education. These certificates were also given for any outstanding contribution to the school (e.g. sports, music, drama). To earn one of these liberally-warded certificates in the first year at school was a goal to which most aspired. Emphasis was put on the reason for the award, not the award itself. In this way it was possible for each eleven-year-old to have 'achieved' in their first year. No failures! Parents were invited, a special guest made the presentation, and the evening ended with refreshments provided by the Northwood School Association. Several of its members with identifying badges, would be there officially to mingle with the new parents, answering queries and disseminating information. Intermingling of staff, parents and pupils was encouraged.

Wednesday 27th: – Busy day at school. Heads of department meeting lasted until 5.00 pm. Governors' meeting 7.00 pm: most interesting. Finished at 10.19 pm. (Fortunately my journey home was a mere three miles.)

Thursday 28th: – Afternoon meeting at Uxbridge Civic Centre. Had to leave a bit early. A good songster practice – finished at 10.00 pm. Worked hard.

Friday 29th: – Hectic day at school, but had an evening in. Very tired.

Saturday 30th: – Got up a bit late. Made a lunch. Evening at Reading Central Salvation Army to 'chair' a songster festival.

Sunday 1st October: – Two meetings. Spent afternoon in bed – so tired! Songsters sang well.

What a week! As Christmas approached, things got more hectic!

Thursday 7th December: – Busy day at school but left in good time. Hendon Songsters participating in the Metropolitan Police Carol Service at Westminster Central Hall. Marvellous turnout: they sang well, Home about 10.20 pm.

Friday 8th December: - Hectic day at school; problems all round. Didn't get away in time to go to my hairdressing appointment. Shopping on the way home. Back to school for the Pantomime – went very well indeed. Hall was full.

Saturday 9th December: - 'Prelude to Christmas' at Hendon Salvation Army. Songsters on duty. Don Morrison played the piano superbly.

Tuesday 12th December: – Very busy day at school. Left at 4.20 pm. Dashed home. Out again to Brent Cross for carol singing with the songsters.

Thursday 14th December: – Meeting at Uxbridge pm. Found time to go to M&S. Evening: back to school for 'Christmas Anthology'.

Friday 15th December: – Very tired today, but not too busy at school. Went back to school for the sixth form/prefects party which went very well. Came home at 9.55 pm.

Tuesday 19th December: – Finished school today. All went well. I caught the 1.45 pm train to visit Freda Youngs (a Hendon songster) in hospital. Did some shopping and window-shopping. Bought a Christmas pudding in Fortnum

& Masons – then had tea and a gateau there. Evening – Staff party at Margaret's.

Thursday 21st December: – Quiet day at home; went to collect with a group of Hendon bandsmen playing at Victoria Station. Lots of police about because of a bomb in Croydon.

Sunday 24th December: – (Christmas Eve). Went to two meetings. Then to Roland and Joan's (Cobb) for supper. Jim and Jean Wilson and Alf and Marjorie Ringham were there. Home at midnight.

Sunday 31st December: – Lots of snow. Nevertheless, got to both meetings. Small songster brigade, but we functioned. 'Happy New Year!'

Looking back I do wonder how I coped with this hectic life-style. It was enjoyable but exhausting. When I retired from school, four terms early, at Easter 1980, I knew I had done the right thing. For the next four years, Hendon Songsters was my only non-domestic responsibility – what a difference that made! From 1980 to 1984 was to be my happiest, and musically the best, period of my work with this fine choral group.

* * *

CHAPTER TWELVE

'Management is the ability to get others to do
what you want them to do'.
(Chalky White)

Northwood School, from four-form entry secondary modern to six-form entry comprehensive dominated my professional life. The transition was challenging, exciting and exhausting. Accepting the first 6-form entry in September – a 50% increase in the number of eleven to twelve year olds – promised to be a major problem; the new extensions to the existing building would not be ready. Having warned the authority about the looming problem, I managed to get away to Plymouth for a five-day break. Then it was back to Northwood. There was no change in the situation: the building foreman agreed that the extensions would not be ready for occupation at the beginning of the autumn term. A call to the education officer in charge of schools was urgent: it would not be easy. Some snippets of the conversation lodged in my memory:

MY: 'We have a big problem. The extensions will not be ready for the beginning of the autumn term.'

Mr R: 'I find that difficult to believe.'

MY: 'I suggest you come to the school and take a look. You will then have no difficulty.'

He didn't come but sent one of his underlings who totally supported my appraisal of the situation. Then followed a meeting with the chief education officer and his assistant responsible for schools. My Deputy, Mr D.J. Edwards was there at my invitation – since the meeting was held in the head teacher's room, I had the authority to invite whomsoever I wished. It was not a pleasant encounter: they seemed to think it was my fault that the new building would not be ready. Surely we could fit an extra sixty pupils into an already bursting-at-the-seams school! Eventually a compromise was reached; at a council building in Northwood there were two spare large rooms: we could use those. Transport to and from them would be provided. When the chief education officer started to tell me how and when to use the rooms, I called a halt to the proceedings:

> 'Leave it with me. We'll make the best possible use of them. Let us hope the new extensions will soon be complete.'

To cut down on time-wasting travel, the two rooms were used for technical drawing and needlework, both of which subjects had three consecutive timetable periods. We also used the school assembly hall for two classes – it was a big hall – and somehow or other everyone coped - that is, until the threat of strike action by the NAS (National Association of Schoolmasters) reared its ugly head.

It was a quirk of fate that the chairman of the school's governing body (a staunch Conservative) was also a strong member of the NAS. He was a Tory, elected chairman in a Labour-controlled council due to an accidental miscast vote. Visiting the school as a union official, he spoke to all the NAS men, and then informed me that if things did not improve quickly, his members would go on strike. A warning telephone call to the education office brought Mr R. to Northwood to speak to the staff – he made matters far worse! I held a series of meetings with the NAS, spelling out the situation and also the damage that a strike would do to the school – we would all suffer! As ever, everyone was kept fully informed of what was happening and the progress being made. I kept my fingers crossed! In the end, the strike threat was withdrawn. It seemed that the NAS men had come to the conclusion that the mistakenly-elected chairman of governors was using the situation for his own political ends.

When I was senior mistress at the Manor School, I had been a member of the NUT. At some point, strike action had been ordered by the union and disruption of the school followed. Personally I was not prepared to withdraw my services, and when I heard the word 'scab' being used, I immediately withdrew from the National Union of Teachers. On being appointed acting head of Northwood School I was able to join the National Association of Head Teachers (NAHT), of which I am now a retired member.

Their advice to me on several occasions was extremely useful and supportive. Towards the end of my career, having been elected president of the Hillingdon branch of the association, I was heavily involved with liaison between head teachers and the local authority, as well as being the head teachers' representative at official functions. I enjoyed that year, but never felt really comfortable when having to confront the chief education officer. He was a brilliant debater, an enthusiastic educationalist but his experience did not include running a comprehensive school. At the end of one of our exchanges, which somehow managed to avoid being acrimonious, I was moved to say,

'Sir, you are more skilled at debate than I. You
will surely win this argument if we pursue it. So
all I have to say is, you've got it wrong'.

In the 1970s there was no national curriculum; head teachers were left to decide what should be taught. They could put into the school timetable any subject provided its inclusion could be justified to the governors and to the education authority. In one school in the borough, Esperanto was taught throughout: the head teacher was an enthusiast. Eventually its unpopularity and uselessness meant that it had to be dropped – how the head teacher got away with it in the first place is beyond my comprehension. When eventually a national curriculum was imposed on us, we found that it was almost exactly what had been developed at Northwood. From my first day at the school it had been obvious that this was no ordinary secondary modern school. The outstanding exam results that year in 'A' level physics proved that the 11+ exam results were not a reliable indicator of future academic performance. When comparing our GCE results with those of the neighbouring grammar schools, I discovered that many of our 11+ 'failures' had achieved more than their contemporaries who had 'passed'. It was important to me that all pupils should have the opportunity to study to the best of their ability, and to have access to all kinds of experiences in sport, drama, music, practical work, athletics, dance, gymnastics, art *et. al.* They needed to know, not only at which subjects they might excel, but also where their weaknesses lay. Whatever else they might or might not experience at school, all pupils should experience a sense of achievement.

From 1971 onwards, the school increased in size annually, eventually reaching a total of 1132 pupils. The raising of the school-leaving age to sixteen and the growth of the sixth form, made a big impact. Coupled with the growing roll was the enlargement of the teaching staff to some seventy-five full timers and innumerable part-timers. The curriculum and the availability of extra-curricular activities developed with the growth of the school. Organisation of teaching groups was discussed at great length and in detail at numerous meetings of senior staff and heads of departments. The final decisions would be mine, but it was essential that I carried the judgment of the people who had to put those decisions into practice. At the end of the day, however, the success or failure of the new system rested with the head teacher. At that time the 'mixed ability' concept of the grouping of pupils into classes was a doctrine being preached by the Labour Party and some educationalists. No child would be in the 'bottom' class: each form group would be an equal spread of low to high IQ pupils. This concept had come to us from across the Atlantic, where I saw for myself the superior facilities – including space and lavish assistance in the classroom – which were essential if this type of organisation were to work. Eventually we were told by the authority that all comprehensive school pupils should be taught in mixed-ability classes. For me, the arguments in favour of this were not convincing. The matter had to be debated fully: all staff opinions would be taken into account before a final decision on organization was made.

This was a very difficult and trying time for me: I had to get it right and carry the judgment of the majority of the staff. Additionally, whatever was put in place, the parents would soon deliver a verdict, as would their offspring. The education authority had not realized that already in all schools many subjects were naturally taught in mixed-ability groups whatever the structure of the timetable: an 'A' stream class could have in it some pupils who had no aptitude for e.g. art and music, whilst someone in a much lower stream might well excel at wood-work, sports and needlecraft . Meetings were held, heads of departments were invited to submit their considered views. After much deliberation, this is what finally emerged:

English	)	Staff prepared to try mixed ability for two
Geography	)	years, then would need to 'set' the classes in
History	)	preparation for examinations at sixteen years.

Mathematics	)	
Modern Languages	)	No mixed ability classes.
Science	)	

A well-established 'remedial' department, with an experienced teacher in charge was allocated another member of staff. Once again fortune favoured us. A former songster of mine from the Harrow days had just qualified as a primary school teacher, but showed interest in the advertised post. She applied for it and got it – Barbara Tinn proved to be an excellent teacher. The success of the department was measured by its losses! There was great excitement when a non-achiever became an achiever! The agreed and stated aim was that the pupils needing this special treatment for the learning of basic skills should be absorbed into the mainstream as soon as possible. When the head of department moved to another school, Barbara was joined by her married sister Rhona – her non-identical twin (also a former Harrow songster). The pupils were never aware of the relationship! This was where my timetable wizard came into her own. She was able to produce a timetable that met the wishes of the staff, wishes which coincided with the conclusions I had reached. Right from the first six-form entry to the time of my retirement, this system met all the needs of the pupils, satisfied the parents and carried the judgment of the staff.

My next big hurdle was how to justify to the education authority what I had done: my report to the governors would soon be due. The directives to secondary schools had not been carried out at Northwood – I was prepared to defend my decision. For mixed-ability teaching we did not have the space, nor the materials. No full-time classroom assistants would be available, nor would necessary new equipment. Finally, the head teacher was not convinced that it was the best way forward.

It took five years for this 'setting' system of time-tabling to be fully operational: despite the directives, we made no changes in the organization already established. Staff, parents and pupils were happy with it. I took a huge risk and decided to leave well alone. In my report to the governors, no mention was made of the structure that had been put in place: the words 'mixed-ability teaching' did not appear. However, I expected the omission to be noticed and for questions to be asked. My preparation for that governor's meeting was very thorough – I was prepared to 'fight my corner'. To my amazement the matter was not raised, no questions were asked nor was mixed-ability teaching on the agenda of any subsequent meetings. The structure that had been developed over the years, with which parents, pupils and teaching staff were happy and which was producing good results, was still in place in 1980, my retirement year.

Early in the 'comprehensive' years I made changes in the curriculum as it affected practical subjects: traditionally needlework and cookery for the girls, technical subjects for boys, with art available to all. Dorothy Youell was presented with an outline of my plans: six core subjects would be needlecraft, cookery, art, woodwork, metalwork and technical drawing. Every pupil in the first two years (11–13 year olds) would spend a term on each of these subjects, after which they could make their choices for years three to five. In this way, girls could try their hand at traditional boys' subjects, and vice-versa. The term 'needlecraft' covered a range of skills, some of which appealed to boys. It is interesting that Brian Turner, the well-known TV chef, wrote in his book *A Yorkshire Lad:*

> 'A crucial turning point in my life came in my third year (at Morley Grammar School). You had to make a choice to take woodwork or metalwork if you were a boy, needlework or domestic science if you were a girl. Three of us boys decided to take

what was then a revolutionary step, and opted for
'domestic science'.'

This is exactly what some Northwood boys did, and a few girls took up traditional boys' subjects. I wonder if any of them pursued these subjects further once they had left school?

At the time of the expulsion of Asians from Uganda, we were told to expect an influx of non-English-speaking refugees. Here was a new and unexpected challenge. Why Northwood? The fact was that Heathrow airport is in the Borough of Hillingdon and as these refugees landed at Heathrow they became Hillingdon's problem. Northwood had quite a number of large empty houses where the Asian refugees could be accommodated and enough schools to cater for the children. Fortunately, we were given several weeks' notice, so we set about making our plans. My first requirement was a teacher who could speak their language and my priority was integration. There were many timetable subjects where the Asian children could be absorbed: physical education, music, all the practical subjects, and interestingly, mathematics. Senior staff and heads of departments worked together to produce a strategy: we had to get it right. Most of these children would be going into the lower school: Miss Ball, head of the lower school, appealed to parents for any item of school uniform in good condition that they could donate. She received it, had it washed, cleaned and stored it – blouses, trousers, skirts, blazers, ties and sports kit. When the Asians arrived, one of the boys was wearing a turban: very soon he was proudly wearing a turban in school colours!

The next priority was language, so all English, history, geography, modern languages and some science lessons were devoted entirely to teaching these somewhat bewildered young people the language of their new home – English, English and more English. Some learnt very quickly and then went into the mainstream; others excelled in sport and practical subjects – any achievement, however small, was applauded. Everybody needs to be seen to be successful!

Occasionally, one of the fathers would come to the school with a query, but we did not see mothers. Our specialist teacher and the school welfare officer visited the homes, and reported back to me that these ladies were more-or-less housebound. Something had to be done! We must get them into school. We laid on transport for these 'ladies in a strange land', brought them to school and into one of the common rooms. Our translator stayed with them and I welcomed them and asked the staff to 'drop in' if they had any free time. The Parents' Association always had a representative present and the sixth-formers were also invited to attend. Tea and biscuits were served, questions were encouraged and over a period of time they were shown round the building. This 'tea-party' became a regular feature of the school week and made a huge contribution to the maintenance of good race relations. Most of all, I wanted them to feel comfortable in their role as parents of Northwood School pupils.

This was more-or-less the start of wholesale immigration nationwide. The Department of Education was showing interest in its impact on the schools. So it was no surprise when two of Her Majesty's Inspectors arrived at the school to look at what we were doing. After a preliminary meeting with me, supplied with a map of the school, and details of classes and rooms they would want to see, they went off to do their inspecting, having been given carte blanche to observe whatever they wanted to see. We entertained them to lunch, and mid-way through the afternoon they returned to my room to discuss their findings. Questions flowed thick and fast:

'Do you have any special Asian days?'

'No.'

'Do these immigrants have their own religious service?'

'No.'

'In domestic science, are they able to cook some of their own national dishes?'

'No.'

Each of these negative answers to these and other questions were stonily received. So I spelt out the school's philosophy: integration not separation, achievement not failure. The staff were happy with this, and the school was free of racial tension and discrimination. The official report of these two 'experts' showed that they were not happy that their ideas were less than enthusiastically received, and as they did not comment positively on the policies we had in place, the report was hardly a glowing one. Fortunately, they had no power to foist their ideas onto us. The success of many of these Asian students, particularly in sport, art, science and mathematics, confirmed the rightness of what we were trying to do. When one of the original 'refugees', having reached the sixth form, was elected deputy head boy, we celebrated!!

In a large school, forward planning and good communication is essential. Each morning at around 7.45 am I pinned a dated daily bulletin on notice boards in the two staff common rooms, the sixth form common room and delivered one to the two deputy heads, the school secretary and the caretaker: this I thought was all that was needed to keep the staff well informed. But a salutary lesson was heading my way. One day, when an after-school staff meeting had been called, a senior member of staff informed me that she would not be there – she could not be expected to stay behind at such short notice. Her after-school appointment could not be broken. This was from a hard-working head of department whose work was exemplary and whose students achieved very high standards. Being challenged like that proved to be a positive thing: only a fool would fail to see her point. The eventual outcome of this incident was that before the beginning of the next school year, each member of staff and all the ancillary staff (especially the secretary and the caretaker) were given a 'Northwood School Staff Handbook'. In it was the calendar for the year (including dates of all staff meetings) and information re. the school's policies. It also included guidelines for the conduct of school journeys and out-of-school activities. Legal requirements as they affected members of staff were also listed.

Henceforward at the beginning of each school year I made a start on the following year's handbook – it was much easier second time round.

This handbook proved its worth over and over again. Never again could a member of staff say, 'I didn't know about it'. Then there were the school journeys – field studies, educational visits, and holidays – there was much going and coming back. The safety of both staff and pupils was of paramount importance: staff were left in no doubt about their professional and legal obligations. One of the rules which was non-negotiable was, 'No drinking (alcohol) and no smoking'. Only one problem arose from this: a father, whose 17 year old daughter was allowed to smoke and drink alcohol at home, felt that her liberty was being infringed. Having explained to him the reasons for this prohibition, I then pointed out that she was at liberty NOT to go on the school journey. The outcome was predictable: she went, accepting the rules and that was the end of that. Some members of staff pointed out to me that these rules and guidance, very specific and spelled out, provided tremendous support if students put pressure on them to be allowed to drink and smoke.

'No! It is as much as my job is worth. Someone is bound to tell the head teacher.'

No news of any infringement of these rules ever reached my ears. In all my years at Northwood there was never a serious accident or incident on any of the school journeys. The school's policy was that all reasonable precautions for the safety of individuals and groups should be taken and be seen to be taken, and that more than adequate supervision should be exercised at all times.

Finance available to the school was based on the *per capita* pattern. The more pupils, the more money, obviously. But also, older pupils as they moved up the school were 'worth' more in financial terms. A big sixth form meant a bigger injection of funds – but of course, a bigger outlay on books and equipment. It was my responsibility to see that the money was well spent and that waste was kept to a minimum. Lighting left on in empty rooms was one of my pet hates! I always kept a contingency fund and made sure that there was some money in hand at the end of every financial year. However, in a forward step, Hillingdon Authority decided to allocate sums of money directly to the head teachers to pay for some ancillary help of their choice. This proved very popular with head teachers, and was expanded over the years. My first choice was to appoint a qualified nurse who would deal with all matters to do with health – medicals, hygiene, vaccinations and supervision of all medical matters. For me, her most important function was dealing with any accidents occurring on the premises and taking appropriate action. If a child needed to be taken to hospital, I insisted that an ambulance be called, and of course, the parents informed. As a teacher on 'playground duty', fear of being called to an accident was very real to me. What had happened? How bad would it be? These thoughts would be in my mind as I ran towards the crowd that had gathered at the scene. For me, having a qualified nurse permanently on a building used daily by some twelve hundred people, was number one priority.

There had been a prefect system in force when I arrived at the school; a head boy, head girl, deputy head boy and a deputy head girl. After staff consultations it was decided to keep this in place. It did mean that some senior pupils were given the opportunity to exercise responsibility, and also, from their meetings, to put forward to the deputy heads some suggestions regarding the day-to-day life of the school. We also established a school council, with representatives from all the year groups and from both teaching and ancillary staff, with a deputy head as chairman. All these activities were run on business-like lines – elections, agendas, minutes and implementation of decisions. Two school council projects stand out in my memory.

1. The mother of two of our pupils was having kidney dialysis for which she had to travel to London.

Obviously, life would be much easier for her and her family if she could have a dialysis machine at home. This matter was raised by a pupil-member of the school council: it was decided that they would ask the school to raise the money! The Deputy Head, Mr

D.J. Edwards chose to associate himself with this project and worked together with the council members. All kinds of schemes were instigated for the raising of money – and it just poured in. We had a 'thermometer' gauge displayed on a wall in a main corridor. Up went the temperature. Before long it had reached the top of the wall. So, across the ceiling it went, and down the other side. Whilst this was happening, there was great excitement in the school, tremendous activity and very GOOD BEHAVIOUR.

Eventually the total amount was raised. The consultant, a Mr Thompson, involved himself in the purchase and installation of the machine, and then came to the school with the mother, to speak to the pupils in both junior and senior assembly. He congratulated the school on the success of the enterprise and the speed with which it had been brought to its conclusion. I believe that every pupil in the school experienced a sense of achievement, and we were all rightly proud how quickly the goal was achieved.

2.   The school council asked for a pay phone to
       be installed for students' use.

They were challenged to investigate: cost, location, security and on-going finance. Having done their homework, they made a strong case for their request to be granted. I was persuaded by their thorough investigations, by the case they presented for the need and by their optimism that it would be properly used and not vandalised. So, once again the wheels were set in motion and the telephone was installed: it was not far from my office so I noted that it was well used. As for problems – there weren't any! It was their phone, they were funding it: all was well.

By the time the first six-form entry had been with us for four-plus years, the school was at its optimum size, apart from any growth in the sixth form. The pattern of the academic work was well-established and the social life of the school was in a healthy state. Extra curricular activities were flourishing. I had remarried and my change of name from Packham to Yendell made headlines in the local press. We moved to a house round the corner from my flat in Hatch End which was outside the school catchment area, but a mere three miles along a main road to

Northwood School. From 1968–1975 my son Andrew was a boarder at Reeds School, Cobham. After 'O' levels, he was given the option of leaving Reeds and going to the local sixth form college. By this time he was enjoying Reeds School – cricket, rugby, orchestra - so he decided to stay, on condition that he be allowed to go to the Hendon Band practice. We saw his tutor – no problem. So every Tuesday evening he left Cobham by train into London and another train to Hendon where Bandmaster Roland Cobb was waiting to give him generous extra tuition on any music that was unfamiliar to him – a 'catching-up' exercise. At ten o'clock each Tuesday evening, armed with food and drink supplies, we picked up Andrew at the Hendon Salvation Army hall and drove him back to Cobham.

I was seeing some big changes in my life, but some things never change.

> 'Yesterday, today, forever, Jesus is the same.
> We may change but Jesus never, Glory to His name'.

Albert Benjamin Simpson
(1843 – 1919)

* * *

CHAPTER THIRTEEN
'Never a dull moment'!

Each day my diary gave details of the expected: the unexpected was yet to be revealed – as on the day when the 'Man from the Ministry' arrived without an appointment. He had come to examine the chemistry laboratory in search of illicit alcohol production. This was new to me – I'd never heard of such a thing! He was taken to the laboratory to meet the jovial Mr Birchall who had no surprises in store for him. When the Inspector came to see me before leaving, I jocularly asked him if he had found the whisky 'still'. He was not amused! So the olive branch in the form of a cup of tea was offered and he left with a handshake and a smile.

People were in and out of the school all day: at that time security was not the problem that it is today. There were several easy access points for people just to walk into the school: it would not have been practical to make the sprawling building secure. Personally, I would find the essential security measures of this twenty-first century very irksome. My policy was to have open access and to welcome people into the school for all kinds of purposes: parents, career advisers, staff from local colleges, police, education officers and advisers, peripatetic music teachers, school health officials, marriage guidance personnel and members of local voluntary organizations. The school welfare officer was a regular visitor, the probation officer less so. As the school was used for teaching practice by the Borough Road Training College and by the Institute of Education in London, we often had visits from the supervising tutors. I remember one afternoon when a Borough Road tutor, who was a Salvationist, met Maisie Wiggins (peripatetic music teacher). They were standing in the rather imposing entrance when Paul Ruby of Hendon Salvation Army and head of music at the school, joined them, and I encountered them in passing,

'All we need now is a flag; then we could have a meeting!' was my comment.

There was the momentous occasion when we actually had the 'Army Flag' on the platform in the school hall. It was speech day and I had invited General F. Coutts to present the prizes and deliver the speech. His uniformed secretary was with him on the platform, and the Hendon commanding officers were occupying VIP seats in the body of the hall. *The Northwood Gazette*'s next edition gave us a good report:

'At Northwood Secondary School, Potter Street, school is more than just lessons, parents were told at the annual speech day on Wednesday, and to prove it, Acting Head Teacher Mrs Muriel Packham outlined the extra-curricular activities that went on in the school during school hours in the previous two days:

'On Monday, we had a visit from some careers officers from the borough,' she said. 'At the same time, our fifth year girls, saw a film on the washing of fabrics, and our fourth year netball team played a match and won.

'On Tuesday, one class went to a neighbouring school to see their presentation of *Arms and the Man* and a boys' class whose PE period it was, went to Twickenham to watch the Inter-Varsity Rugby match.

'Today, a combined staff-pupil soccer team played a match against the London College of Divinity, and I'm delighted to say we won 4–0.

'The academic achievements of the school continue to be high,' said Mrs Packham. 'In fact, three students – E. Hopper, M. Stonehill, and T. Stower – each gained nine GCSE's'.

Guest speaker was General Frederick Coutts of the Salvation Army. He urged pupils not to take their education for granted, and cited three places he had visited where 'To attend school is a Christian privilege, and where there is a real thirst for knowledge'.

'I visited The Salvation Army School for the Blind in Jamaica,' said the General. 'Although the children are all sightless, I was greeted by a Calypso band and by a school orchestra.'

The second school he mentioned was above a tenement in Hong Kong. Here the demand for education is so great that two schools operate every day – one in the morning and one in the afternoon. Each is attended by up to five hundred children. The third school was in Papua, New Guinea, where General Coutts saw men of giant physique bending over books and learning 'things which we learned when we were six or seven years old'. General Coutts concluded,

> 'We must never forget how privileged we are to
> have the education we have.'

From General Coutts to a young Salvation Army officer stationed at Uxbridge is quite a leap. This young officer rang for an appointment to see me about a boy in his Sunday school. With the pupil's file in front of me, I greeted him as he came into my room and offered him a seat – every visitor, even an irate parent, was a VIP. Clearly, the officer had some concerns about the boy, but at school he was not a problem. My visitor was very impressive – he had 'done his homework' and made his case with clarity. However, he had not done any homework regarding the head teacher: Over a cup of tea I told him I was the songster leader at Hendon – he was somewhat 'gob-smacked'.

Sometimes we would be asked to consider accepting a pupil from some other school in the borough. One such request featured a girl who needed a safe, controlled and caring environment which she was not getting at her present school. Would I see the parents? The implied compliment in the question guaranteed an affirmative answer. Details were sent to me: the name seemed familiar. As soon as the parents entered the room, I recognized them: the bandmaster of a nearby Salvation Army Corps and his wife who had been at many of the early 'singing company camps' at Sunbury Court, first as a student and then as a sergeant. What a lovely surprise! When in 1998 we had a re-union at Sunbury Court to celebrate the fiftieth anniversary of the first singing company camp, that mother was there. I was delighted to see her and to hear that her daughter, who had done very well at Northwood, was settled in a job in a happy and caring environment. Then there was the Probation Officer: Vic Ashworth from Harrow Corps. He knew whom to expect as he walked into the head teacher's room. Once we had dealt with the reason for his visit we were able to have a cup of tea and a chat. My secretary had a limitless supply of the necessities: a cup of tea, like the proverbial oil, helps to 'make the wheels go round'.

In response to a request for an officer to visit the school to talk to my religious education class about the work of the Salvation Army, Captain Jorge Booth was sent. (At my insistence, some teaching was always on my timetable and I usually taught the less popular [with the staff] groups of pupils.) Representatives of other religions and faiths had been to talk to this group of boys – now it was the Army captain's turn. An older boy had been sent to Northwood Hills station to meet our visitor.

'How shall I know him?'

'He'll be in Salvation Army uniform'.

All was well. He arrived safely and gave a very good lesson. Had he been a teacher I wondered? The next week, in class discussion, someone asked,

'Can we have the Salvation Army man again?'

He was 'top of the pops'!

Our policy regarding visitors was that they should be shown to the school office; any strangers on the building were directed to the school secretary. Information about expected visitors was published on the daily bulletin, and teachers were encouraged to challenge any stranger in the building. One day, a man walked towards me on the top corridor. The pile of books I was carrying became unstable and fell to the floor, scattering wildly. As I knelt to pick them up, the man approached me.

'Excuse me, could you tell me the way to the head teacher's room?'

'Yes, I could.'

So I stood up and pointed him in the direction whence he had come, giving him a rather circuitous route to my office – he thanked me and retraced his steps. I grabbed my books, and having hurriedly taken the shortest route to my room, was serenely seated at my desk when he was shown in. Surprise, surprise! I smiled,

'I believe we have already met!'

He saw the funny side of the encounter and we both laughed – then business, then the cup of tea.

A 'panic' button which could summon help had been installed in my room: one never knew what to expect. It was needed on only one occasion. A somewhat aggressive and unstable sixteen year old was 'on the carpet'. His eyes had strayed to a large pair of scissors on my desk – they were within his reach. Casually – at least I hoped it appeared casual – I got up from my desk and walked round to place myself between him and the scissors, at the same time pressing the 'panic button'. The office was never left unattended, so I was sure of a response. It came in the form of a knock on my door and,

'Mrs Yendell, I must remind you that you have an appointment . . .'

The interview was suspended, to be continued at the end of afternoon school, when the deputy head would be with me.

I was always pleased to welcome the authority's advisers to the school: in some schools in the borough they were merely tolerated. To me, they were an additional resource, and I often needed their advice on subjects of which I had very little knowledge. Mr Nicholson, of the Saga holiday episode (as mentioned in chapter one) was someone on whom I relied for advice and help in the technical studies department. When a Mr Jim Craddock was appointed as senior adviser to the authority, I immediately contacted him and invited him to visit us. Northwood School was on the outside northern edge of the borough: no-one ever called in to see us *en passant*. Some head teachers are suspicious of advisers but it was in everyone's interests for them to be given opportunity to do just what their title implied – give us the benefit of their expertise and experience, and to monitor the work of the various departments. Mr Craddock became a good friend to me and to Northwood School. At a later date he came to the Salvation Army at Hendon to compère a songster festival.

A Mr Stephenson was appointed music adviser to Hillingdon and I was anxious to meet him. Music and the other arts are important aspects of a school's life and support and help from these subject specialists was important. He later agreed to appoint Paul Ruby, a Salvationist from Hendon, to the post of music specialist. A vacancy for a music teacher had been advertised and interviews were held, but no appointment was made. Thereafter, Mr Ruby's position was explained to the adviser: as a member of a Guard's band he had taught in prisons and as a peripatetic music teacher, but he was not qualified to take a full-time post in a state school. So the adviser agreed to interview Paul. As he was a personal friend of mine, and as Mr Stephenson's judgement was to be trusted, I opted out of the appointing process at that stage. The adviser's first words to me after the interview were,

> 'I like your Mr Ruby. I'll go back to the office,
> look at the rule book, and see how much we will
> be able to offer him.'

Obviously the offer was reasonable, because Paul accepted the post as an unqualified teacher and was put in charge of the subject throughout the school. Later he took a year out to do a course which would give him his qualified teacher status. I was a bit concerned that he might not come back, but he did return and was soon officially head of the music department with an enhanced salary. I was not convinced that the year out had made much difference to Paul's performance in school: still 'outstandingly good'.

The music department soon established a programme of instrumental teaching with the help of several peripatetic teachers employed by the borough. Maisie (Wiggins) worked with Paul for several years – it was a personal pleasure for me to have her coming into school; the pupils were getting top-class tuition. All the teaching – mostly at the end of afternoon school – was geared to Associated Board of the Royal School of Music Examinations. So many pupils were involved in this tuition, that we were able to have the AB examiners come to the school, instead of our going to the examiner. It was quite difficult to ensure a quiet place for the exams, but we managed it.

My policy of making sure that everyone – teachers and pupils – knew what was to happen during the school day proved its worth in these circumstances. Morning assembly was a good opportunity for me to deal with this. So, at both junior and senior assembly the pupils were told about the forthcoming music exams, where they would take place and the importance to the school and the candidates of the need for absence of noise. I also expressed my certainty that this could be achieved – they would be helping their friends who had worked so hard for these exams.

Even away from school one could not always get away from school. A few years ago, at the annual 'Hendon Highlights' Festival at the Queen Elizabeth Hall on the South Bank, an interesting encounter took place. During the interval, my friend went out of the hall, leaving an empty seat between me and a man to my right. He started up a conversation,

'Excuse me, are you Mrs Yendell of Northwood School?'

'Yes, that's right. Should I know you?'

'Well, I know you. I once came to your school for an interview for a teaching post.'

'Oh dear! You didn't get it, did you?'

'No. But that's all right. I got another one soon afterwards.'

'Oh good! I'm glad about that.'

'Small world' are the words that spring to mind.

I always felt sorry for interviewees who were not appointed; and of course one can never feel absolutely sure of the rightness of the decision made. 'Time will tell', and it did. On one occasion I was desperate for a PE teacher for the girls – I had failed to make an appointment when interviewing: if one is not sure, it is better not to appoint than to make an irreversible mistake. I had soon learned that 'no teacher is better than any teacher'. The PE adviser rang me. She had been interviewing at another school: only two candidates. Would I like to see the unsuccessful one who had made a good impression at her interview? My first reaction was 'If she's not good enough for Barnhill School, she is not good enough for Northwood.'

Then common sense reminded me that the adviser was to be trusted. So Faith Rowbottom was interviewed – and being very impressive, was appointed there and then. She was as good as any PE teacher I had ever observed. Later she told me that she was very pleased not to have been appointed to the first school. So was I! Her specialty was dance, and from then on until she left, dance became a prominent part of the physical education syllabus, and featured in concerts, open evenings and other events.

Technical studies staff were always in short supply. At one point we desperately needed a woodwork teacher. A very nice young man applied – the only applicant. By that time, I had developed a procedure for interviews. First I would meet each applicant briefly, then pass them on to the deputy head to be shown round the school. They would then meet the second deputy who would discuss the syllabus, timetable and general organization of the school. The head of department would also meet the applicant. Very rarely were there more than two applicants to be interviewed for the subjects where there was known to be a teacher shortage. After all that, the applicant would be waiting to see the head teacher with the subject adviser. On this occasion, Mr Nicholson had already seen him and thought that he was a good candidate. So, the young man, a Mr Moss,

163

came in to see me. He was unusual in that he had a degree – something new in the technical studies field. This was to be his first teaching post. He was pleasant, articulate and obviously knew his subject. The question was, would he be able to manage groups of boys in an environment that – in the interests of health and safety – required strict discipline? DJ (Deputy Head) had similar doubts, but on balance we decided to take a chance and offer him the post. To my amazement, he asked for a few days to think it over. He was given a mere thirty minutes with DJ to make up his mind: that did the trick – he soon returned to my office to accept the post of woodwork teacher in the technical studies department.

On a new teacher's first day, I would usually visit their classroom/workshop to ask if they had everything that they needed, and then after a few days for them to settle in, another visit would be paid. They needed to know that they had the support of all the senior staff. The woodwork shop was a single-storey building outside the main part of the school: it was important for me to check how things were going there. Some three days into the new term, as I approached the room there were no signs of activity – no hammers being used, no machinery in motion. Through the glass upper part of the door an interesting scene could be observed: boys standing to attention behind their work benches, and a strong authoritative voice in full flow. So I knocked and went in: Mr Moss was 'laying down the law' in no uncertain terms. He glanced at me, I signalled to him to carry on: it was music to my ears! Any doubts I had harboured about discipline were immediately dispelled. That teacher's control of the woodwork room was total and as time went on, the standard of work and exam successes were excellent.

Included in my Chamber's Dictionary under the heading 'discipline' are such phrases as:

'An ordered way of life'.

'The state of self control achieved by training'.

In this twenty-first century it seems to me that discipline is a 'dirty' word: it has unpleasant connotations. My belief is that in teaching, whether in a classroom, on the sports field, in the band practice or a choir rehearsal (songster practice), without discipline (i.e. order) the results achieved will be on the 'plain' rather than the 'mountain top'. Discipline does not have to be unpleasant. Children especially will never forgive unfairness – and we all have something of the child in us, whatever our age. *How to be a successful choir director* [written by John Bertalot, published by Kevin Mayhew, 2002] would make useful reading for anyone involved in teaching – especially chapters two and three. In chapter two he writes:

> 'Discipline can be fun. Singing is fun, playing the
> organ is fun, conducting can be fun – and they all
> need discipline'.

On the exchange visit to the USA, I was taken to a lecture given by an eminent sociologist. His subject was, 'the child, the adolescent and the adult'. All of us have in our make-up characteristics of each, but in different ratios. Some adults have a lot of the child in their persona, whilst some children display the attributes of adulthood, as do some adolescents. Who has not, at some time or other, wanted to say to a childish adult, 'Be your age'? This rather obvious concept was new to me, but it proved to be invaluable in my dealings with many and varied characters who came my way. A benevolent discipline is essential to learning and reaps its reward not only in good examination results but also in excellence in other fields – e.g. sports, drama and music.

In Hillingdon, Northwood's results in Associated Board music exams were always at the top of the Borough's order-of-merit list. At one head teachers' meeting these results were being discussed:

> 'You are lucky at Northwood: you have a lot of
> musical children'.

'My luck is in having a brilliant music teacher who can work miracles'.

Paul was a veritable 'Pied Piper'. I had to admit to my colleagues that some parents applied for their children to come to Northwood because of the music, just as other schools attracted pupils for some specialism in which that school was particularly successful.

One day I had a telephone call from the director, asking me if I would agree to Paul Ruby being 'borrowed' for two days by another school. An official re-opening of the school was to take place, but the scheduled music was by no means ready for performance – they needed a Mr Ruby. My first thought was that it would create a difficulty at Northwood as his work would have to be covered by someone else, who would then lose a free period. The loss of a teacher's free period causes annoyance and sometimes resentment, as I had discovered at the Manor School when it was my responsibility to provide cover for absent colleagues. However, this was a huge vote of confidence in Paul's teaching ability, so I spoke personally to every teacher who had to cover one of his lessons – they were all remarkably tolerant, and saw this as a 'feather-in-the-cap' situation for our 'Pied Piper'. Two days and he transformed the choir and the orchestra: the school's music teacher had my sympathy.

When at a later date we ourselves were having an official opening as a six-form comprehensive school, I was surprised by a visit from a junior education officer. He explained that he had been sent to check out the music for the big day! Poor man! No-one had told him that he need not bother – the music at Northwood would be fine. Mr Stephenson had obviously not been apprised of the visit – he would have warned off the unsuspecting young man. As gently as I could, I explained that there was no need to vet the music. When he tried to insist (he was only doing what he had been told to do), I explained that I was not prepared to take pupils out of lessons for a pointless exercise, but assured him it would be 'all right on the night', and it was! That official opening brought me once again into conflict with the director of education. A buffet supper for all the guests was being prepared by the domestic science department (now food technology); soft drinks followed by coffee were to be served by the senior pupils in attendance. A message from the director informed me which alcoholic drinks were to be provided. To me, as a Salvationist, this was a problem. My views were conveyed to the director, but he insisted and actually provided the wines himself. Even head teachers cannot always have their own way!

The time came for Paul Ruby to move on – he changed from being head of music at Northwood to being teacher in charge of the instrumental work in the Borough of Hendon. We were all sorry to see him go, but fortunately I was able to appoint Des Vinall to the post: he had just completed the year's teacher training available to qualified musicians and was able to carry on where Paul left off. After one year he left us for a head of department post; a well-recommended Mr R. Stewart applied for the position and was appointed. All the advisers came into the school from time to time – if by appointment, they would report to the office and then go off to see the teachers concerned. If not by appointment, then they would see the head or the deputy head before doing anything else. We always needed to know who was on the premises. Vigilance by staff and pupils was encouraged, and anyone wandering about the school would certainly be challenged. When, some years later I went to a school in the East End of London to examine some music students taking practical music exams, it was difficult to get into the school: there was only one unlocked gate onto the premises, all the doors into the school were locked, with just one bell to be rung by visitors. The door opened, and was locked again – it seemed like a prison to me. It was a relief when I finally left the school to make my way home.

Mr Stephenson, the music adviser, was appointed 'pastoral adviser' to Northwood School: he was my direct link to the education office. We were both happy about this. He often came to see me on non-music matters: once these had been dealt with, the conversation usually turned to music. He knew that Paul Ruby, Maisie Wiggins and I were all involved in Salvation Army music-making, and also that music had been my special subject. He recognised that Northwood School was making a big contribution to the Borough's orchestra and choir; in return, he performed a brilliant piano recital at one of our lunchtime concerts, using the grand piano in the school hall. A huge audience of pupils and staff gave him a standing ovation. This was the sort of thing I encouraged – staff and students joining together voluntarily in their spare time. Good relationships within the school were very important, and the good will engendered by shared voluntary activities spilled over into the classroom to the benefit of both staff and students. It helped to 'oil the wheels'.

Meanwhile, my dual involvement continued – the school and The Salvation Army.

* * *

CHAPTER FOURTEEN
'Whenever people are making music together,
at that time they are better human beings'.
(Yehudi Menuhin).

'Hendon Highlights' is a well-known annual musical 'feast' early in the new year at the Festival Hall. However, Hendon Songsters had some highlights in their annual calendar. A dictionary definition of 'highlights' is 'the most memorable moments', and Hendon Songsters certainly had plenty of those.

From 1978–1984 was an action-packed era for us; we travelled extensively. Nevertheless, I have always been convinced that a songster brigade's prime function is to serve its own corps and, unless it can do that well, it cannot justify 'specialling' at other corps. As songsters we must make a 'spiritual' contribution at home before we consider weekends away and participation in prestigious Salvation Army Music Festivals – these are merely a bonus. I know I carried the judgement of the songsters on this point: their week-by-week commitment was tremendous.

Good choral singing mattered to me and to the members of Hendon Songsters. Was it the only thing that mattered? Indeed not! As a teacher with music qualifications directly related to choral work, I had no option but to go for the highest standard we could possibly achieve. The better the singing, the more effective its impact on our listeners. For songsters, there is no greater joy than to see someone, moved by the Spirit, making his/her way to the 'mercy seat' as they are singing.

When we were the 'solo' brigade for the Sunday evening meeting at a London bandsmen/songsters councils' day, Commissioner Dalziel (British Commissioner in those days) asked me if we could sing something suitable as the prayer meeting progressed. *O disclose Thy lovely face* [words by Charles Wesley, music by Commissioner Mrs Sven Tyndal] was the song I chose. The impact was electric – soon many of the Songsters/Bandsmen were kneeling at the front of the meeting room. We must have sung it at least ten times. The words of the last verse are very powerful:

Visit, then, this soul of mine, pierce the gloom of sin and grief:
Fill me, Radiancy divine, scatter all my unbelief;
More and more Thyself display, shining to the perfect day.

Not only the listeners, but also the singers were conscious of the Spirit of God in that prayer meeting. I recall a young Salvationist who was part of a small group talking together about Salvation Army choral music. I was giving my views on the need for high musical standards. I sensed that he was not happy with them. His question to me proved that point,

'How often do you have a spiritual meeting at your Hendon Songster practice?'

I think he was hoping to prove that we were not as spiritual as we ought to be!

'Every songster practice,' was my reply.

How can a group of Salvation Army singers rehearse songs such as *All that I am*, [words and music by Bill Himes] without being aware of the Holy Spirit in the singing thereof?

All that I am, all I can be,
All that I am, all that is me,
Accept and use Lord as you would choose Lord
Right now, today.
Take every passion, every skill,
Take all my dreams and bend them to your will,
My all I give, Lord, for you I'll live Lord,
Come what may.

This is just one of the Salvation Army songs the singing of which makes us aware of the presence of the Spirit of God.

In 1998 I visited Cape Town at the start of a round-the-world journey. The songster leader at the Salvation Army Corps rang me before I left home,

'Will you conduct the Songsters on Sunday morning?'

'I can't. I won't have my SA uniform with me.'

'That's all right.'

'I can't do it without a rehearsal.'

'That's all right too. I've called a rehearsal for 9.15 on Sunday morning.'

'What are you planning to sing?'

'Ivor Bosanko's *His Provision* [words by John Gowans].'

'Oh! Well then, the answer is 'Yes'.'

So that Sunday morning in South Africa, after an early rehearsal which they all attended, I had the great privilege of conducting the Cape Town Songsters as they sang that most powerful song. During the singing of the second chorus:

Holy Spirit, promised presence fall on me,
Holy Spirit, make me all I long to be.
Holy Spirit, Holy Spirit,
Give your power to me, Holy Spirit.

there was an acute awareness of the presence of the Holy Spirit. A young man, singing tenor, left his place in the songsters, and made his way to the 'mercy seat'. We carried on singing. How can anyone challenge the usefulness of songster brigades, and how can they criticize the songster leader who studies to be 'a workman that needeth not to be ashamed' when the singing's spiritual impact is so often thus confirmed? The same song was used at Bristol Easton when I was there for the songster weekend. I arranged for the last chorus to actually be a prayer: no conducting, all eyes closed. It is not possible to describe in terrestrial terms the spiritual impact of the last moments of that holiness meeting.

Over the years I have reached the conclusion that unconducted singing in rehearsal immediately improves the cohesion of the choir. Why? Could it be because the singers have to rely on their own listening skills to achieve? Listening requires a mental effort and without a conductor the need to THINK is evident. Without thought the singing is mere production of given notes and words – no music, no message. On one occasion the Hendon Songsters were at Reading Salvation Army as guests with Eric Ball as compère: he was a very special person and we were honoured that he was there. Early in the programme – prayer time – we were to sing the setting of *The Lord's Prayer* by John Larsson, but at Thursday's songster practice we had run out of time without rehearsing it. So instead we sang it as a benediction: no conducting, all eyes closed – we prayed it. On the way home I said to my husband,

'I wish I had the guts to do it like that on Saturday.'

'Why not?' he asked.

At Reading, I suddenly decided we would risk it. As we gathered together for prayer before the start of the meeting, I told the Songsters what we would do – no copies because eyes closed. The five beats of the piano introduction was in the safe hands of Elaine Cobb – that was all we needed. THINK and PRAY was the order of the day. I stood with them and sang – very nervously – thinking, 'What have I done'? There was no need for nerves – it was a really lovely and moving prayer. A lady whom I had met at the Salvation Army Training College some weeks previously was in that meeting. She wrote to me later. Because of listening to me speaking to the cadets, she had decided to hear the songster brigade – to check me out. Apparently she had very much enjoyed the evening:

'But for me, the highlight was the singing of the Lord's Prayer at the beginning of the meeting', she wrote.

Singing in cathedrals must surely rank as a 'Highlight' for any songster brigade. When we visited Coventry for a weekend, we were taken to the cathedral, but the outstanding moments were when we stood around the preserved ruins of the original cathedral which had been destroyed during a blitz on Coventry in the 1939-1945 war. Crowds gathered as we sang, unaccompanied, *Grant us Thy Peace*, [words by Ivy Mawby, and music by George Marshall], *In the Stillness*, [words by Commissioner R. Woods, music by George Marshall], and *Jesus answers Prayer*, [words by Ivy Mawby, music by Alistair McHarg]. A scripture reading and prayer preceded a sung benediction: those were hallowed highlights.

Some years ago I went to Guildford SA to hear a songster brigade from Plymouth (Songster Leader Terry Neilson). This group was unusual in that it had no pianist, which meant that most of their work was unaccompanied. The beautiful sound and immaculate ensemble work was testimony to the value of unaccompanied rehearsal and performance. Terry had borrowed a pianist for the weekend, who was used only when a song had an independent piano accompaniment. If I could pass a non-negotiable rule for songster leaders, it would be 'Some unaccompanied singing in every rehearsal and in public at least once every two weeks'.

When Hendon Songsters were invited to Peterborough for a weekend, there were to be two Saturday services in the cathedral – a formal service in the afternoon and a 'music praise' in the evening. It was freezing cold in the cathedral in the afternoon, so much so that we had to wear our overcoats, except when we stood up to sing. In my collection of unpublished vocal music I have a beautiful setting for SATB of the words attributed to Bernard of Clairvaux (1091-1153):

Jesus the very thought of Thee with sweetness fills my breast;
But sweeter far Thy face to see and in Thy presence rest.

Bruce Broughton wrote the music, which was not at all easy to learn or to sing. We worked hard at it, and the joyful experience of hearing ourselves sing it unaccompanied in that beautiful building was unforgettable. This same song was used again in 1983 at the Territorial Music School, where with a group of about twenty students, I formed a four-part choir, which was the forerunner of today's 'A' chorus. It was important to get a good balance, so I asked for tenor and bass volunteers and then restricted the number of sopranos and altos. Among the men were Bobby Irvine, now well-known as a vocal soloist, and some young men from Croydon who later formed themselves into a very good male voice quartette – Mark Bearcroft, Gerald Boniface, Jonathan Byfield and Iain Parkhouse. We rehearsed in whatever spare moments we could find. These young people sang beautifully at the Wednesday evening festival, and Norman Bearcroft immediately said he wanted it on the Saturday programme – more rehearsals needed! 1982 was my first time at the Territorial Music School since the amalgamation of the two single-sex schools. Having been to several of the final festivals, I could not understand why mixed voice singing was not featured: why not a major work? Early in 1982 Norman Bearcroft rang me:

'I have some good news and some bad news; which do you want first?'

'I'll take the bad news.'

'Sorry I cannot allow Hendon Songsters to sing *Lord we know that we love you* at the National Songster Festival'.

'Why not?'

'It isn't published.'

'But the Salvation Army has published it in Australia.'

'Sorry, you can't do it; it isn't published in this country.'

'O.K. Now what's the good news?'

'We would like you to come to the Territorial Music School to do the singing.'

'I'd love to come, and I will come, but on one condition.'

174

'What's that?'

'That the whole school sings together something written for SATB voices.'

'Well, you'll have to do it yourself.'

'That's all right. I'll do it if you wish, but I don't really mind who does it, so long as it is done.'

Thus it was that in 1982 the Cobham Chorus made its debut, singing *This Age of Rockets,* [words by Jack Izzard] written specially for the occasion by Ray Steadman-Allen. It was a tour-de-force, with the choir finally declaiming in the words of F.R. Havergal and to the tune *Rachie:*

> *By Thy grand redemption,*
> *By Thy grace divine,*
> *We are on the Lord's side,*
> *Saviour, we are Thine.*

That same year Hendon Songsters had been invited by the Metropolitan Police Band to sing at their annual carol service at Westminster Central Hall; we must have given a good account of ourselves because we were invited again the following year; it was to be held in St. Paul's Cathedral. This really was something special. I was aware of the problem of 'echo' in that vast cathedral and wondered how we would fare. Hazel Renshaw, who was the songster sergeant at Hendon at that time, wrote:

> 'The acoustics are famously difficult in that church, the sound coming back to the singers a few seconds after they have sung, so great care has to be taken in the choice of music to be performed. We joined with the Police Band to sing the *Hallelujah Chorus* from Handel's Messiah, and the sound of the 'Hallelujahs' resounding around the cathedral was thrilling.'

There is always some tension for everybody concerned when being involved in a 'big occasion'. Hazel suffered some embarrassment that evening:

'I was caught in a traffic snarl-up on the Finchley Road and was therefore late! The policeman on duty outside the cathedral took great pity on me when he saw the state I was in, and allowed me to park right outside the door. My embarrassment increased when I had to walk the length of the nave and take my place on the front row. I then discovered that one epaulette was missing from my shoulder. My seatbelt had caused it to be detached and it was later found in the front of my car'.

Hendon Songsters' visit to Blackpool Corps was another memorable occasion – we sang in the famous Tower Ballroom which was filled to capacity. At such times it is important for the conductor to radiate confidence and calmness however stomach-churning the situation might be! Always nervous, I tried not to show it: we had prepared, we had prayed – all would be well! Now was the time for me to inspire them to sing better than they had ever previously done! Not that these big events were more important than our visits to small corps or our contribution to the meetings at our own corps. Anything and everything we did mattered, whether it be in a Salvation Army hall or in a cathedral. Of our visit to Sheffield Hazel Renshaw wrote:

'Our weekend at Sheffield Citadel was memorable too, as several seekers were recorded in our Sunday evening meeting – a humbling and also thrilling experience for us. The purpose of a Salvation Army songster brigade is not only to bring to people wonderful music, but also to impart the Christian message of God's Love and forgiveness and the possibility of a new life in Christ'.

One day in the early 1980s I had a telephone call from Kath Dolling, the commanding officer of Chesham Corps. Recently I met her at a Home League Rally. Did she remember? She certainly did, and when I asked her if she could write something about the occasion, this is what she sent to me:

COMRADES IN CRISIS (Or Hendon to the rescue).

'In the early 1980s, whilst stationed in the Chiltern Hills, the market town of Chesham had given generously to The Army's Self Denial Appeal. As a gesture of thanks, we decided to put on a musical festival in one of our central churches and accordingly booked a prestigious London band for this event. Imagine our dismay when with all the tickets out, just a week before the event they 'phoned to say they had inadvertently double-booked and would not be coming!

'My hot-line to the Lord instructed me to give a certain Muriel Yendell a ring to see if there was any possibility that her songsters could come to our rescue.

'Just let me put it to them at rehearsal tonight', she said. With less then a week to go, 'Happy to oblige' came the wonderful reply.

'But the following Saturday night (although being at the end of April) brought a severe snowstorm. Just to try our faith, I guess, because the gallant songsters braved the elements (and with our basin-steep hills it was courageous) and the church was packed to the gallery to receive their excellent presentation No charge was made for admission, but COMPLIMENTARY tickets brought their own reward, with overflowing offering baskets. Praise the Lord, and heartfelt thanks to Muriel and her minstrels'.

Kath Dolling.

Easter is a very special time for songsters – there is such a wealth of beautiful music available. For several years at Hendon, we presented a Good Friday evening programme of music and readings: some of the choral work was traditional music from *The Messiah* [G.F. Handel]. A big favourite of mine was the *Passion Chorale* by Hassler: there are three verses, and the second verse is harmonised differently from the other two. Musically, to sing through the three verses unaccompanied, and to reach the last chord absolutely in tune with the first was quite an achievement. It is a beautiful 'Passion' hymn, moving for both songsters and listeners.

In 1981 I decided to do something more ambitious. Stainer's *Crucifixion* is a larger work, requiring a mixed voice choir, two principal male soloists and some other male soloists for minor roles. It would have to be performed on the Saturday before Good Friday for practical reasons. Ideally we would need a church organ and an organist to go with it! The two principal soloists were not difficult to find: both my first choices agreed to come: Elgar Gambling (tenor) and Peter Laing (baritone). It was suggested that we could hire an electronic organ, but I didn't think the composer would approve, and nor did I! Church organ it had to be or we could not do it. Don Morrison, a former Hendon Bandmaster, had a son who was the organist at the Hendon Parish Church, and was the music critic of *The Times* newspaper. My friend Marjorie Ringham had been his piano teacher. I knew that Richard was well-disposed towards the Salvation Army. (He had written the foreword for my book *Let them sing*.) When I had a chat to Don, he was sure that Richard would be willing to help, but insisted that I ask him myself. Well, I did – I re-introduced myself, said what I was planning and asked what chance there was of using the Parish Church, the church organ with the organist 'thrown in'. Richard was keen to do it (the dates were fortunately clear) and a formal request in writing to the vicar settled the matter.

Having got as far as the planning, and having borrowed sets of music from a local music library and started work on the choruses, I suddenly thought 'How about a guest conductor?' The first and only name that sprang to mind was Eric Ball – I was sure he would come if he were free on that Saturday. Yes, he could come; yes, he would be pleased to come to a Friday evening rehearsal and stay over at my home for two nights. We worked hard on the chorales. Richard came to the Thursday evening songster rehearsal and Eric arrived on the Friday for an evening rehearsal in the parish church as did the visiting soloists. Adjusting to the acoustics of the church and to the organ accompaniments, we had a long, but extremely interesting rehearsal. All other arrangements for this special evening were left in the capable hands of the Songster Secretary, Pauline Varnals: with Pauline nothing was left to chance! Eric Ball conducting Hendon Songsters was a dream come true. The songsters were inspired to produce their best work, as were the soloists. For me it was an extra-terrestrial experience. This event was the Hendon highlight of all highlights.

Immediately after Easter, I received from Eric a letter that I treasure:

'Dear Muriel,

I want to thank you and Bill for so kindly entertaining us in your home during our recent visit to Hendon. It was good to be in touch again and to hear something of your music-making, and we particularly enjoyed the 'Three Ems' get-together. (The 'Three Ems' were Marjorie [Ringham], Maisie [Wiggins] and Muriel [Yendell].)

My own part in the presentation of the Stainer work was for me most rewarding because the songsters were so well prepared and responsive. They seemed to react quickly and, indeed, 'professionally'. I found the actual performance to be a moving experience, and so did Olive, who is an experienced listener.

I was fortunate to be working with a sensitive organist in Richard Morrison, and of course the soloists did very well also. So to you Muriel, my thanks for inviting me and congratulations on what you are achieving with your choralists. My thanks to them all. Once more – thanks to you all at home. Bless you.

Yours sincerely,

Eric (Ball)'.

At that time, Easter 1981, I was doing my best work with Hendon Songsters. Could it be because at Easter 1980 I had retired from my headship? My last two years at Northwood School proved to be very hectic and I had been feeling the strain: I can remember the exact moment when I knew it was time to retire.

* * *

CHAPTER FIFTEEN

'If all were easy, if all were bright,
where would the cross be, and where the fight?
But in the hardness, God gives to you
chances of proving that you are true'.
(Lucie Booth-Helberg)
Salvation Army Song Book No.773

Once a school timetable is working properly, it could be imagined that everything would then go smoothly. Not so! To think that would be wishful thinking. A community of some twelve hundred and forty people was not a train running on well-oiled wheels! The reality was that every day was different; most days brought some drama, some mishap and something quite unexpected – like the day when the local police descended on the school having received a warning that there was a bomb on the premises. The school had a very well-rehearsed 'fire drill' which immediately went into over-drive, meeting the time-target for total evacuation and roll call. With all personnel assembled way out on the school field, and every individual accounted for, I joined the police as they searched the premises, trying not to show my alarm. There was no bomb: the 'all clear' was given and everyone went back to work – most of them had enjoyed the excitement. Who was the culprit? Who had rung the police? DJ and I immediately looked at the registers and chose to scrutinize those where we were likely to find the names of known miscreants. Sure enough, our main suspect was marked absent: a girl who was a well-known prankster. The fact that whilst the police were in the school building the tyres of their cars had been deflated convinced us that we had found the culprit. She was a large, loud, likeable jolly girl whose sense of mischief was only matched by her fearlessness. Of course she was in serious trouble with the police, who knew her well.

We did however have a 'real' fire in the school! A small room near the school hall was used to house costumes and props belonging to the drama department. Francesca Annis, a well-known actress, had a nephew and niece at the school. One day, they came to see me with an offer from their aunt – she was having a clear-out of theatrical costumes – would we like to have them? We certainly would! Space was at a premium but it was obvious that we needed a 'costume and props' room. So a small room in the corridor which ran alongside the school hall was cleared out and handed over to Mrs Bray, the drama teacher. Not long after this, smoke was seen coming from under the door of the 'props' room; the alarm was raised, the Fire Brigade called and the school evacuated. At the time it did not seem to be in any way a dangerous situation, but risks were not to be taken. It is better to err on the side of caution than to have to say later, 'I thought it would be all right'.

We had actually got the fire under control by the time the Fire Brigade arrived – very little damage was done. At the time, the play *Pygmalion* [G.B. Shaw] was being produced and the strikingly good-looking head-boy was playing Professor Higgins. The fire revealed a sad tale: a girl, who was not at all prepossessing in appearance, had a crush on 'the professor', but he wasn't even aware of her existence! So this was her way of getting his attention – setting fire to the costumes. It was not a crime; it was a cry from the heart!

It was not all doom and gloom! Johnny Speight, the celebrated writer of the well-known TV series *Till death us do part*, had a son and daughter at the school. When we needed someone to declare 'open' the summer fete, he offered to bring the well-known Dandy Nicholls who played the mother in the series. The Northwood School Association organized and ran these fund-raising social functions most successfully, roping in parents who could offer something unique. One of the Berni brothers of Berni Inns fame always brought a huge decorated cake to be raffled at these events. (He usually brought a small one for the head teacher!)

A member of staff who taught car maintenance was a vintage-car enthusiast. Bob Wood was a charming person who had a wonderful relationship with his students; I sometimes thought that vintage cars was his work and school was his hobby! Most of his weekends were spent on the continent at car rallies: it was quite a while before I realized the reason for his occasional Monday morning absences – he'd missed the last boat home! Something had to be said – he took the hint and increased his efforts to get back for the start of Monday morning school. He and one of his cars spent the whole afternoon of one summer fete giving vintage car rides round the huge playing field, thus raising lots of money for school funds. His hectic weekends on the continent provided an amusing incident; at the end of a Monday afternoon school, two fourth year boys went to see John Levermore, head of middle school. Their story was that towards the end of the lesson Mr Wood had 'dropped off to sleep'. When the bell rang for the end of afternoon school the class had decided not to disturb him, but to leave quietly and to let Mr L know what had happened!

I usually arrived at school about 7.30 am. Steve Cobb – at that time a student teacher and now head of the Salvation Army's Music Ministries Department in the U.K. Territory – told me that during his final teaching practice at Northwood School he at one point determined that he would get to school before I did. So he tried – but did not succeed. That must be his only failure to date! Some staff said that seeing my car there when they arrived was reassuring: that was nice to know. What I never did know was what would be waiting for me when I got there.

One very cold Monday morning the caretaker met me to say that the boilers were not functioning and therefore the school was extremely cold. She had already contacted the appropriate person at the council offices and someone would be sent out to us as soon as possible. In the meantime, what? We, the senior staff who were always in early, decided to tell everyone exactly what the problem was and to say that coats, scarves etc. should be worn until the problem was solved. There was nothing else we could do – business as usual had to be the order of the day!

Fairly early after the start of the school day, I received a message to say that four boys (fifteen-year-olds) were going home as the temperature inside school was below the legal limit for factories! DJ had intercepted them and was bringing them to see me. The small electric fire which I kept in my store room and which at that point was helping to keep me warm was hastily 're-stored'. The four boys came into my room: we had quite a discussion. What was their problem? Wasn't it the same for everybody? Wasn't this an opportunity to learn to cope with a bit of discomfort? As they were determined to go home and as I could not physically prevent them from doing so, I advised them that on reaching home they should turn on electric fires, make hot drinks and settle down to a nice comfy morning. In the meantime, those made of sterner stuff would put up with the cold knowing that everything possible was being done to get things back to normal.

'Go home! Go home now!' I said.

They looked amazed and then turned to leave the room.

> 'Just one more thing. When you return to a nice warm school this afternoon, you will first of all report to me and you will CRAWL into this room! Is that clear?'

The consternation on their faces was almost comical. I opened the door for them to leave and they walked out. They didn't go home (I checked) and the heating was soon restored. I had a telephone call from the local press later that morning:

> 'We hear you have a strike at Northwood.'

> 'Really, what gave you that idea?'

> 'We had a telephone call to say that some pupils were going home because you have no heating.'

> 'Yes, the heating was off, but it is on now. I can assure you that no pupils have gone home. You must have been misinformed. Sorry! No story!'

I was somewhat annoyed about the press being brought into it but decided to take no further action – the episode had reached a satisfactory conclusion. 'All's well that ends well!'

On another occasion as I arrived at school, the caretaker, Mrs B, greeted me with the news that on all the classroom doors along the 'top corridor' slogans had been daubed. It had obviously been done by present-day pupils: the aptness of the painted comments was proof enough. Mrs B had already moved some of her cleaners onto washing the classroom doors: those senior staff (including me) who were already in the building joined in and we had removed every trace of paint before the pupils came into the building. That morning was senior assembly day; as I took my place on the platform, I could sense an anticipatory deep silence – somebody was waiting for my reaction! They waited in vain! I had early in my career realised that the more fuss one makes about such incidents the more delighted are the miscreants. No harm had been done, nothing was damaged and, more importantly, the efforts of some rascals to cause trouble and to gloat about it, had been frustrated. They must have been very disappointed! A second 'mini-strike' occurred when a group of four girls, who were seated at the far corner of the field, refused to come into school after the morning break. The staff on duty had tried to persuade them but failed. So the problem came to 'the-buck-stops-here' lady! I strolled across to where they were sitting, thinking as I went that I just HAD to get them in with no fuss. Actually their problem was such a minor thing that I cannot remember what it was all about. I do know that I persuaded them that until they came into the school to talk about this problem, nothing could be done. I would just simply have to leave them there. They quickly decided to return with me to the school building and later a satisfactory resolution was reached.

Sometimes, in spite of all that was done to help new teachers to settle in, someone would be having discipline problems in the classroom. There was always help and advice available – heads of departments, senior staff and even the head teacher. I regularly visited classes of new staff. One young man was obviously continuing to have problems with a group of pupils. We discussed the matter and I suggested some tried and tested ways of dealing with such situations. When I'd finished, he looked at me and said,

'I can't do that.'

'Oh, why not?'

'It's not me. It wouldn't work for me.'

'Well, fair enough! BUT you yourself then will have to find the way. You MUST.'

So I left him to do just that; eventually, he had taken control of that group and his discipline problems were over.

Another young teacher, like her colleague, had trouble with just one class. She was very worried – they were noisy and disruptive and she was at her wits end. I had seen her teaching Spanish to other groups and she was doing really well. She had also shown initiative in arranging for her class to go for a meal to the local Spanish restaurant. The proprietor had a daughter in school and he was prepared to put on an early evening meal just for us – provided only Spanish was spoken. I went with them and didn't understand a word they said.

To try to solve her problem, we worked out a strategy for dealing with this disruptive class. She would get their whole attention by telling them that she did not want to teach them anymore – she'd had enough of them: the head teacher needed to know. She would then send a reliable pupil to my room to ask me to go to the classroom as she, Mrs B, needed to see me. I would go to the classroom with the messenger, apparently thinking that something pleasant was happening. The plan was that Mrs B at that point would tell me in no uncertain terms what she thought about this class, and that she did not want ever to see them again. We kept up the charade – 'Please reconsider'. I apologized for their rudeness and bad behaviour, and expressed the hope that they had not fallen too far behind the other classes in that age group. She agreed to reconsider, and to give me a weekly report on them. I thanked her for her willingness to give them another chance. They took the offered reprieve and that was the end of that! No more trouble, lots of work and they began to enjoy it!

I was sometimes involved in music activities where I would play the piano for choir rehearsals. Several of the staff were permanent members of the choir and Mr D.A. Edwards was an excellent pianist who was prepared to do the piano accompaniments for the public performances. One Tuesday, when for that evening's concert we were giving a performance of *Hiawatha's Wedding Feast*, Mr D.A. was on sick leave. We rang his home – no, he would not be able to come to the concert. There was nothing else for it: I would have to play. Every minute between arriving home from school and getting ready to go back for the evening concert, was spent at the piano – practising. I had to go back early because Elgar Gambling (Regent Hall Songster Leader) was singing the tenor Aria and we needed to get together to run through that. It was all very nerve-wracking for me. A note was on my desk the next morning:

> 'You just took over and played the entire thing
> perfectly – we were proud of you.'

At a later date, the writer – Juanita Levermore – stepped in as the leading lady in the school's performance of *Oliver* when the student due to sing the part, lost her voice. No dull moments, but many stressful ones!

The 'lost' exam paper created something of a crisis. We had what we thought was a foolproof system for the secure storage of exam papers prior to the exams and for the collection and posting of the completed papers thereafter. The question papers were kept in a locked safe in my office; at the end of each exam the scripts were collected by the invigilator and the senior member of staff responsible for the whole of the administration of the CSE exams. (This was before GCE and CSE amalgamated to produce the GCSE). A telephone call I received from the CSE Board was a shock – an exam paper was missing! Both teachers involved in collecting, checking and posting the papers were 'up-in-arms'. They had done their job properly: all papers had been checked by each of them independently, parcelled ready for posting with the invigilator observing, and then posted – a certificate of posting was produced. All the agreed rules had been meticulously followed. I called a meeting of senior staff plus those involved in any way with that exam.

What more could be done? Discussions with the exam board were fruitless. The invigilator felt threatened. As no one was being accused of anything I couldn't take that too seriously. Finally and unbelievably, I had a telephone call from the exam board – very apologetic, almost grovelling – the 'lost' paper had been found, and they accepted full responsibility. Immediately I gave the good news to my deputies and called the other staff involved to a meeting in my room. At first the atmosphere was rather frosty. Even before I had the opportunity to speak, the members of staff most involved were voicing their protests – they seemed to feel that their professionalism was being challenged. Nothing was further from the truth – they were both conscientious and reliable. So cutting them short, I told everybody that the script had been found: the relief was palpable. The only thing I could do was to insist on a letter of apology from the examination board.

Christmas was always a busy time at school. We had two important events: the Christmas review for the whole school arranged by the lower sixth – two performances on two afternoons, and the evening 'Christmas Anthology' for parents and visitors arranged by the upper sixth. I personally vetted the contents of the afternoon concert. The pupils were a captive audience and it was important that there should be nothing in the concert to which even the most puritan of parents could object. Those who planned and organized these concerts knew what was required – good, clean fun. The staff would always be subjected to a certain amount of wry humour, and the head teacher was not excluded! On one occasion I was fairly graphically portrayed by a senior girl who was chastening a youngster; she 'brought the house down' when she said in a very good imitation of me:

'Look at me when I'm talking to you!'

At my last Christmas review, I had the chance to be the perpetrator of the joke. In a *Diamond Jubilee Northwood School Magazine* published in 1994, my successor as head of the school, Mr N. Chapman wrote:

'. . . Northwood was the job I wanted. When I visited the school before the interview I had immediately been taken by the atmosphere, the friendliness and the warmth of the welcome. My first 'Official' visit, at the invitation of Mrs Yendell, was to the Christmas anthology: this confirmed my original impression, and for this reason in particular, the anthology remained one of my favourite evenings on the school calendar.

'My second visit was a few days later when I went onto the platform at the end of the Christmas review to be introduced to the school, blinded I might add, by a spotlight courtesy of Mr Meade, (Technical assistant) shortly after Mrs Yendell had landed a well aimed custard pie on the face of the head boy!'

'The Christmas anthology was the 'highlight of the winter season',' wrote David Hood in the same magazine. 'This was the responsibility of the upper sixth and I as their form tutor, helped organize it. For me, Christmas began on this evening in the decorated halls, with the carols, the items by the choir and orchestra and the seasonal readings from the lectern, chosen and read by the students. The finale for the evening was always the *Hallelujah Chorus* – parents would bring their copies of the *Messiah* and join the school choir and staff for a robust performance.'

HALLELUJAH!

* * *

A card from Gill and Heather (Hendon Songsters) to me, in hospital 1984

Adult Music School September 1991

Cruising with Jimmy Saville 'All work and no play makes Jack a dull boy'

Time out in the Yorkshire Dales

Husband Bill at home with a young Marianne and Michael

Maunday Service with family in Westminster Abbey

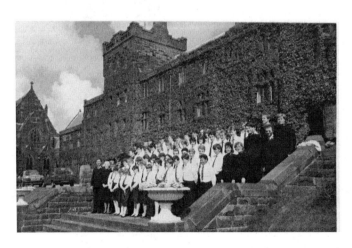

Manchesters Division's Music School

*50th Anniversay Reunion Singing Company 'Camp'
at Sunbury Court 2nd-4th July 1998*

*50th Anniversay Reunion
Colonel Brindley Boon being persuaded to conduct his song:
'Such a lovely world He made'*

Persuaded!

June Collin – The Peerless accompanist.

Staines Home League Singers 1988

Staines H.L. singers at the opening of the new hall

*Staines Fellowship chorus Christmas lunch at
Sunbury Court 1999 . . .*

. . . and in the Conference Centre.

*With General John and Commissioner Gisele Gowans
at Music Leaders' Conference July 2004*

CHAPTER SIXTEEN
'Patient endurance attaineth to all things'.
(Teresa of Avila)

As on a previous occasion, two girls who, having gone to sit down on the school field in the corner furthest from the building, decided not to return to classes after break. Some persuasive teacher was needed to, at least, get them back into the building. This time I asked the teacher on 'playground duty' to do it.

> 'I don't have the answers anymore,' was my comment.

That made me think seriously about retiring early: when I did retire in 1980 at Easter, I had been in the school for over fifteen years and for fourteen years and two terms had been the person in charge – responsible for everything and to everybody. With one thousand, one hundred and thirty-two pupils on the roll, some seventy-five full time teachers, numerous part-timers and all the ancillary staff (e.g. laboratory technicians, technical assistants, caretaking, cleaning and cooking staff) it was a very big community. In 1978, I had been elected President of the Hillingdon Head Teacher's Association, which I felt to be a great honour. It meant that I chaired all the meetings, was spokesperson for the Head Teachers' Association at consultation meetings with the education officers and with the elected representatives on the borough council. It was a very busy time, interesting and most enjoyable. The chief education officer moved on in 1979 and it was I who had to make a speech at a farewell meeting. As his conversation and argument had always been littered with quotations, I suggested that the obligatory 'leaving present' should be a book of quotations: I rather enjoyed that presentation. During the year, I had to attend numerous events in my official capacity, including the president's dinner, which we held at the London Zoo – in the restaurant there of course! The National Association of Head Teachers held their annual conference at Norwich and it was my duty to attend. The highlight for me was the service in the cathedral: the conference itself was interesting but hardly riveting.

Northwood School was always over-subscribed, but I did once accept an extra ten pupils late in the summer term of 1977. The chief education officer rang me and greeted me very cordially. My suspicions were aroused – what did he want, I wondered! His story was that he had a group of angry parents whose children had not been given places at their first choice school – a very good school near their homes. They were steadfastly refusing to accept places in the school to which their children had been allocated. A heated discussion had ensued, the outcome of which was that the only alternative school they were prepared to accept was Northwood. Wow! It must be admitted that in view of my rather unsatisfactory previous encounters with the chief education officer, I determined not to be too eager to help him out.

'Mrs Yendell, can you help us?'

'Well, we've already got a full intake for September.'

'Is there any way that you could fit these people in?'

'Would I be entitled to an extra member of staff?'

'Yes, certainly.'

'In that case, I'll look into it and let you know later today.'

When I discussed this with my 'timetabling' deputy head, she thought it would be possible, provided we were given an extra teacher. One factor in the situation was that parents who were prepared to 'dig in' on the matter of their children's education would be supportive of the school. So it was that the deal was done; ten extra pupils, generous additional funding, an extra teacher and a grateful chief education officer – it made my day! My hunch about the parents proved to be right: their children were hard-working and co-operative, and the parents gave 100% support, some becoming staunch members of the Northwood School Association.

I had mixed feelings about retiring early, and yet was mightily relieved when the decision had been made. It was when Mr Chapman was actually appointed to follow me that I realized that my resignation was a fait-accompli. Strangely enough, the burden of responsibility seemed to lighten as Easter 1980 drew nearer. But there was another burden looming that I had no intention of abandoning. Hendon Songsters were booked to do a six-day tour in the Netherlands. Sixty of us were going – Thursday evening, through to the following Wednesday. There had been much planning, a lot of work and fund raising. However a huge problem re. transport had reared it ugly head. One of the Hendon Songsters worked at IHQ in the travel department and she was given the task of making bookings for our flights. She assured us that it had been done; we would fly from, and arrive back at Heathrow Airport. We would however have to transport ourselves to and from the airport. Then, suddenly in February, panic stations! The ever-vigilant Pauline (songster secretary) was worried because neither confirmation of booking nor tickets had been received. She had been assured that the booking had been made. A telephone call to the S.A. travel bureau, who then contacted the travel company, confirmed out worst fears – there was no booking. The company found a record of receipt of our money, but both the money and a travel company employee had disappeared! Fortunately, I had a half-term holiday, so was able to visit IHQ to see the manager of the travel department: at my request he had summoned two representatives of the air company that was to fly us to Amsterdam. My husband was in the insurance business so I picked his brains and made notes about our rights, their responsibilities and the actual form of words I should use.

We had an interesting discussion at IHQ. An offer of seats on two planes departing from Heathrow, one four hours later than the other was refused, so was an offer of an early evening flight from Gatwick – I knew that some songsters would not be able to get there in time.

> 'How about leaving from Luton – no charge for
> the coach!'

Now we were getting somewhere – Hendon to Luton Airport is fairly straightforward. It seemed that the form of words suggested by my husband was bearing fruit.

> 'We have a brand-new seventy-five-seater plane at Luton. You could travel to and from Amsterdam on it: no other passengers. A coach to and from Luton would be provided.'

That was it! The deal was done. It was a brand-new plane, we had our own private jet, and there was no need for the stewardesses to switch on the 'No Smoking' signs! Once again we had an example of what seemed at the time to be a setback, turning out to be a blessing in disguise.

The Saturday before Easter, we had a very special event at the Hendon Salvation Army – a Dutch evening. The Dutch Embassy had arranged for some of their girls, dressed in their national costume, to come to the festival with flags, displays and goods which were typical of their country. The hall was suitably decorated and the Ambassador for the Netherlands joined us for a wonderful evening. I personally had very little to do with organization of the event – the singing was my responsibility: not that anything was left to chance.

> 'Muriel was a head teacher (as I was) and she used to get the songster locals together for frequent 'staff meetings'. This was a very useful strategy as we were able to plan the way ahead for the brigade, discuss important issues together and share out the tasks.'

> Hazel Renshaw

A young man named Dick Krommenhoek had visited Hendon Corps a few weeks before that Easter. He and a friend had come to 'check out' this songster brigade that was due in Holland. It so happened that the band was away specialling and I had decided to sing an unpublished piece *Morning Song* [words and music by Eric Ball] that had been written for a National Songsters' reunion at Hendon. It is beautiful, and has since been published for mixed

198

voices. From that point on, Dick became a Hendon Songster 'fan'. He met us as we arrived at Schiphol Airport and accompanied us wherever we went. Some months later he brought his Rhythm Group to England, visiting Luton Temple; a crowd of us from Hendon went to hear them, and gave them the Dutch sign of approval – standing to applaud to show our appreciation.

On our Saturday visit to Dordrecht we did not get the standing ovation until well into the programme. We were to sing a group of songs from *Spirit* [words by J. Gowans, music by John Larsson] which we did with piano, percussion and some brass accompaniment. I remember miming to the songsters before we started to sing:

'Make them stand!'

Singing to an audience/congregation is all about communicating. At the end of the last song, 'What does the Spirit say?' the singers really do have to ask the question: singing the notes and the words is not enough. Each listener should feel, as the singers sing the final 'to you', that it really is a personal challenge. Long before we had finished singing, the congregation stood and the applause that followed the final chords was tumultuous. They had got the message and we had been given the ultimate sign of approval.

Major David Guy – a former commanding officer at Hendon, came with us on the tour. He was well-known and well-liked by all of us, and his preaching was par excellence. As songster leader I had a good relationship with David which survived an incident when he refused a request I made to him. The order of things at Hendon was that the band sat in the body of the hall on Sunday mornings and on the platform in the evenings. The songsters were always on the side of the hall, never on the platform. So, one Sunday morning I asked David if he would mind if the songsters used the platform.

'Yes, I would mind.'

'Why, what's the problem?'

'I do not want half of my congregation behind me when I'm preaching.'

That seemed a good enough reason to me, so we stayed where we were.

Many years later, when chatting to David, I asked him if he remembered the incident.

'When you refused to let us go onto the platform on Sunday mornings, you could have knocked me down with a feather.'

To which David replied,

'And when you accepted that, you could have knocked me down with a feather.'

Of this incident, David wrote:

'Most section leaders would have said, "Well, they are expecting to go on the platform" or "I have told them that we might do this and it will be difficult to go back on that now" or even "having persuaded me to become songster leader you might at least back me up," (after which the CO caves in, leads the morning meeting badly, complains bitterly to his wife over the dinner table and does not recover the joy of his salvation until half-way through the evening meeting)'.

In the same letter, to my surprise David wrote:

'Now do you remember passing on to me a poem by your mother in Nelson about coming to terms with old age? I still have it. Twice in the poem your dear mum refers to being seventy-three. As I am now pushing seventy-three her faith and philosophy have become more than a good verse to share with an elderly congregation, especially the last two lines.'

Grandma's Poem.

Sitting alone as I often do
Thinking my own life's story through,
I think of all God's gifts to me
That still are mine, though I'm seventy-three.

I can see to read, when bright the light,
Listen to the wireless many a night,
I can write, I can sew or make a gown,
It's only my memory lets me down,
And my friends will say quite cheerily
What can you expect at seventy-three?

There is something in that, though I feel it so
When I want to hurry I must go slow.
But I'm not redundant, I do what I can
And leave the rest for God to plan.

Maggie Wilson.

The tour went like clockwork – no hitches, no lost luggage, no missed coaches. A morning spent at the Hilversum Radio recording studios was interesting – we were very well received. I was told that it was a good recording: certainly the technicians seemed very pleased, and we were finished before the end of the allotted time. Unfortunately, for some reason, we did not receive the promised tape of the recording. I wonder what happened to it. Surely we should have followed that up? Twenty-three years on is probably too late, but . . .

My last term at school was remarkably peaceful. All systems and procedures were well-established and things ran as smoothly as could be expected in a society of over 1,200 people. Over 1,100 of these were obliged by law to be there until the end of the term in which they reached sixteen years of age. When the school-leaving age had been raised to sixteen, it was a mixed blessing at Northwood. Already 82% of the pupils were staying on to take GCE examinations. Amongst the 18% who were now legally required to stay in school for an extra year were some very

201

reluctant teenagers. This was a problem we had to address – a way must be found to make their last year both relevant and satisfying. With some pupils we did not succeed. They were in school, they did not want to be in school and it showed! However, after a year or two, this attitude had disappeared as the new school-leaving age ceased to be 'new' and became the 'norm'. The certificate of secondary education (CSE) was introduced at that time and became a worthwhile goal for some of these pupils. Our system of 'setting' for academic subjects meant that a mix of the two exams was possible: each GCE pupil could have a tailor-made timetable to suit their strengths and weaknesses. Without the timetabling wizardry of Dorothy Youell (second deputy head) this would not have been possible.

The advent of computers into homes and especially into the office and workplace caused me to explore the possibility of putting 'computer skills' onto the school curriculum. I advertised for a teacher and made a bid for a classroom to be turned into a computer room. Both these initiatives were successful and we were soon able to offer computing skills as a fourth year option. There were no examinations available in the subject, but it was possible to ask an examination board's permission to write one's own syllabus and prepare examples of the sort of examination papers that would be set. The Board then had to validate the exam: it was quite a long process. I rang a head teacher friend, Edgar Mitchell, whose school was in a neighbouring borough. He was a good friend; we had met quite often at Salvation Army functions. All this led to my visiting his school and meeting his computing skills teacher. They already had in place a CSE mode three syllabus and they were extremely generous in giving me copies of that and of sample examination papers. The Northwood teacher modified that syllabus to suit our needs and we applied to the CSE board for permission to register the mode three exam, submitting copies of the syllabus and sample examination papers. When we received approval we were in business!

A large school is such a busy place and yet I can remember that my last term was relatively calm. I kept in touch with my successor and gave him all the information he needed to take over the running of the school – he would have to get the timetable done in the summer term – not my job any more. Hallelujah! He came to Northwood to be involved in the appointment of a member of staff for the following term and he was invited to attend whatever functions he chose. I finished any outstanding business and was quite ready to go by the end of term. There was a sense of unreality about it. Of course, a 'leaving party' was organized with invites having gone to education officers and advisers; D. J. Edwards had the task of asking me if there was anything special I wanted for a 'leaving present'. That is always a difficult question to answer. I could hardly ask them how much money they had to spend! So I decided on some china: 'Royal Doulton Mosaic Garden'. My thinking was that however little money was collected they would at least be able to buy a couple of cups and saucers! They gave me a lovely early evening party, refreshments by courtesy of the domestic science department. As for the china, it was eight pieces of everything – tea cups and saucers, three sizes of plates, cereal dishes, fruit dishes, tea pot, milk jug, sugar bowl, gravy boat, coffee cups and saucers, coffee pot, small jug and sugar bowl and finally two lidded vegetable tureens. I was overwhelmed: and then I received generous gifts from the Northwood School Association and the pupils themselves. It was a lovely occasion. Throughout all the procedures and 'last-time' events, I felt no regret at my decision to retire. Being at Northwood School had been a wonderful end to my teaching career: I had given it my best shot and it was time to go! There was no time to think about it anyway.

My last school day was a Tuesday: On the Thursday I was off to Holland with the songsters. Thinking well ahead, I had decided that I wanted to do something special on the first day of the next school term (a Tuesday). Very often, and especially when I knew that a tricky problem was waiting for me at school, I had been tempted, as I drove up Potter Street, to go on straight past the school. But of course, I couldn't. So we booked a short holiday in the West Country, commencing on that Tuesday. Setting off early, we followed my route to school and turned into Potter Street at about 8.50 am. Some stragglers were making their way slowly towards the school – and we DROVE STRAIGHT ON!!! Not my problem anymore! I had retired; the Holland tour was history and now I was going to have a life of leisure, - so I imagined. How wrong could I be?

* * *

CHAPTER SEVENTEEN

'Day by day, the promise reads,
Daily strength for daily needs'.
(Josiah Conder)

Never at any time did I regret retiring early, but the dream of an easy life with lots of leisure time proved to be a snare and a delusion. There is an adage that declares that 'Work expands to fill the time available': its truth was about to be proved. Almost before I realized what was happening I had become my husband's typist and bookkeeper – my commerce course of 1938 was still proving useful! Then there was the phone call from a former colleague, asking me to consider doing one-day-a-week's teaching (music) at his school – a Roman Catholic comprehensive school in Ickenham. It was tempting; only one day, music and payment! I agreed. In theory, I would work five and a half hours for which the remuneration would be at the hourly rate prevailing at the time. The reality was quite different. My teaching day started at 8.30 am and did not finish until 4.45 pm!

8.30 am – Two girls for singing; they had been entered for Associate Board Singing Examinations.

9 am to 12 noon – Class teaching.

12.15 am to 12.45 pm – Junior choir practice (Speech day was looming and something had to be prepared for that event).

1.30 am to 3.30 pm – More class teaching.

3.45 am to 4.45 pm – School orchestra, with which I was required to help.

In certain subject lessons, it is possible to take a breather whilst the class gets on with some reading or writing. Not so with music! After some weeks of this madness, I spoke to the head teacher about my impossible timetable; he immediately offered to reduce my teaching time by one hour.

To my amazement and chagrin, I did not find the classes easy to manage. They had lost their trendy guitar-playing young man teacher only to find themselves with an old lady! (So it seemed to them.) The head of music was a great performer and entertainer; he reserved his serious music teaching for the school orchestra, which was very good. Privately, I rather sympathized with the youngsters who were having me inflicted on them! It was my job to teach, not just to entertain. So for the first time since my early days at Whitefield School, I really was challenged. Accepting that challenge and winning the day was extremely hard work.

The lunch-time choir practices were fine. For speech day I prepared three Joy Webb songs: they were always popular in schools, especially *Hand me down my silver trumpet, Lord*, and at Christmas time, *A Starry Night*. The next problem was that this newly-formed choir had never sung in public: it was essential that they should have a 'trial run' before taking to the stage at a public, prestigious event. So it was arranged for them to sing at a morning assembly – this proved to be on a day when I would not normally be in school: another round trip of about sixteen miles! A pre-assembly run-through at 8.00 am had been arranged – as ever, my work was expanding. As we practised Joy Webb's songs I smiled to myself at the thought of Salvation Army songs being performed at a Roman Catholic School assembly and speech day. All went well on the night. These twelve and thirteen year-olds sang their hearts out and 'brought the house down'. That was my school-teaching swan-song. I had told the head teacher that a one-day-a-week commitment was not for me – it was not my style. He was very disappointed and I felt I had let him down – that was not my style either. Occasionally I was later asked to go back to Northwood School to invigilate exams, which proved to be a much easier assignment.

My involvement in education continued as an examiner in practical music for the only GCE Board offering such an exam at that time. At Don Osgood's suggestion I had applied to do this seasonal work and was called for an interview. Over the years I had conducted countless interviews: to be on the other side of the table was somewhat nerve-wracking. I need not have worried: the chairman did all the talking – I listened and answered the very few questions that came my way. Without more ado, I was appointed and arrangements were made for me to have some training. From then until 1984 – my *annus horribilis* – I enjoyed this new kind of work. At the same time and in the same way, I became an examiner for CSE English – both oral and written work. It was most enjoyable and as it was summer work it did not impinge on my other activities. Marking the English scripts was very agreeable: the surprise to me was that the scripts told me something about the teaching. Each batch of papers was unique, revealing a) intelligent pupils taught by a good teacher, b) as a) but a poor teacher, and c) not very intelligent pupils who had obviously had a very good teacher. That was so interesting! One could always spot good teaching.

Early in 1981 my husband and I went to Bognor Regis for a weekend, and on the spur of the moment, bought a flat! At the time it seemed to be a bit mad, but later events proved it to have been a good move. Situated at the top of a Victorian house in a terrace that faced the sea, it was an ideal holiday home. A lovely lawn bordered by a low-level stone wall separated us from the promenade, the beach and the sea. The living room, kitchen and bedroom on floor two of the building had a panoramic view of the sea, whilst the two bedrooms on floor three looked out over the tops of nearby houses towards the Sussex hills. It was lovely: we spent a good deal of time there when our Salvation Army commitments would allow: not Sundays of course, nor Thursday evenings when we had the Hendon songster practice.

It was from March 1980 to March 1984 that I felt I was doing my best work with Hendon Songsters: having no Northwood School responsibility, I had more energy – both mental and physical – to give to the task. I had always enjoyed working with the Hendon folks – but this period of four years was the 'icing on the cake'. We had a pleasurable relationship with the King's Singers of that period; Bill Ives had been my son's music teacher at Reed's School. Both he and Andrew's house master had been to Hendon SA for a music festival. Hendon Band had presented a programme at one of the school's regular Saturday evening concerts and Commissioner Will Pratt had preached the sermon at a Sunday morning service at the school.

A Christmas Concert given by the King's Singers at the Barbican was a regular feature on the social calendar. Pauline (songster secretary) did the organizing and a crowd of us would go: since I knew Bill Ives it followed that we got to know the other singers – they called us the 'Hendon Salvation Army crowd'. Nigel Perrin I later met at another function and suddenly decided to ask him if he would come to Hendon to do a rehearsal with the songsters. He readily accepted and in response to my enquiry said,

'No fee!'

What a songster practice! It was long, but it seemed short – almost two hours and yet we sang only two songs. The bulk of the time was spent on a beautiful song published by the Salvation Army, *O Holy Mystery* [English text: T.N. Rive, music: T.L. De Victoria 1548-1608]. We were soon given the order, 'Coats off ladies; jackets off, gentlemen'. We were standing for long periods of time; most of the singing was unaccompanied – we really did have to think and listen. It was the most interesting, exhausting and rewarding rehearsal I have ever experienced. We used that song on many later occasions – singing it made everything else seem relatively easy! Every choir should sometimes work on music that challenges and stretches them, but not totally beyond their ability. It calls for judicious choice of music by the songster leader. I was once at a songster festival where I noted that very same song was on the programme. After hearing the choir's opening song, I knew that *O Holy Mystery* would be way beyond them – and so it proved.

Bringing in 'guest conductors' to songster practice was another way of keeping things interesting. When Chris Priest, Peter Ayling and Kevin Norbury were 'up and coming' composers, I invited them to a songster practice to tell us something about their songs we were currently learning and do some work on them with us. Unfortunately, Peter was unable to come, but we had a most enjoyable time with Chris and Kevin.

When later Songster Leader Eric Sharpe of Danforth Songsters (Canada) visited us, he too was called upon to participate in the songster rehearsal. Again it was most interesting and stimulating.

The years 1980-1984 were very happy for me so far as Salvation Army music activities were concerned. My two visits to the Scottish Music School were memorable: I was so privileged to be invited to be the music director at the 1982 and 1983 Schools. Major Doug Rayner was the youth officer in charge and I had asked him to arrange a staff meeting on the first Saturday afternoon – that was my way of working; meet everybody, plan the week ahead, and ensure that everyone knows what has to happen and what their own responsibilities will be. After that, the thing should run like clockwork. We had our meeting, chaired by Major Rayner. All was well until we started to discuss the organization for the bands – should we have an 'A' and a 'B' band or would it be better to create two bands of roughly equal ability? A good case could be made for each of these alternatives. All the men involved with the bands joined in the discussion which threatened to become somewhat heated, as I sat quietly listening. Then came the point when Major Rayner called a halt to the discussion and asked for my comments.

> 'Well, gentlemen, I have been listening very carefully to what you all have to say. After I have given the matter due consideration, I will let you know my decision.'

One could have heard the proverbial pin drop. Perhaps it was a bit imperious, but there was no time to waste on endless arguments. So we moved on to other matters.

I was introducing something new into the programme: SATB singing in which the whole school would participate. For this I would need total co-operation from the men on the staff – any of them not joining in the massed singing would be giving out the wrong signals: singing is not for boys/men! When I told them what I planned to do, they all immediately gave me their full support verbally, and were as good as their word throughout the week. They also graciously accepted my decision re. the bands: an A and a B band.

The Childhood Suite by Ray Steadman-Allan was my choice for the 'big number'. Its first performance was at the Royal Albert Hall 'Councils Festival'. Having heard it, I asked RS-A if I could have a copy and we worked on it at Hendon, and even put it on our LP record, on which occasion RS-A himself was conducting. It is written with a very taxing piano part, and also has flute and percussion accompaniment. When I told Elaine Cobb, the Hendon pianist, that we were going to use the *Childhood Suite* she was astounded.

'I can't play that!' she exclaimed.

'Yes you can. You'll see – you'll do it.'

And she did – brilliantly!

Before going to Scotland, I had contacted Major Doug Rayner, asking the vital questions:

'Do you have a good percussionist?'

'Do you have a good flautist?'

These were non-negotiable requirements, one of which was already met – the percussionist. I knew David Henderson, who was to be the school pianist: he would be able to manage the piano part. I took Elizabeth Renshaw with me – an excellent flautist. It so happened that she was in the Hendon Songsters' timbrel group: preparing a timbrel display for the final festival was added to her list of responsibilities. The only problem remaining was that a young man was needed to sing a solo verse of *A little ship was on the sea*. I didn't ask for volunteers – that could have created problems. (I have always believed that it is easier to prevent problems from arising rather than try to solve them afterwards). So I asked the young men present to let me know if they felt someone could and would sing that verse. They soon had their suggestion ready.

'We think Bobby could do it.'

'Oh, (looking at the group) which is Bobby?'

'Over there' they pointed.

'Ask him to come and see me'.

So Bobby came.

'Do you think you could do it?'

'I'll have a go.'

And that was how I met Bobby Irvine, whose career as a soloist I have followed with great interest and satisfaction. He came to the Territorial Music School in 1983 and was one of that small group who worked with me on some SATB unaccompanied songs. I encouraged him to get some professional coaching. He well recalls that first solo:

'I remember waiting for a sign from the conductor – then I was to step forward and sing my verse . . . It was a time of setting standards, especially for young people: new and more challenging music was becoming available. At that music school, great emphasis also was placed on vocal technique, which for many of us was news, news which was not altogether appreciated by some of the boys. Using her skills as an assertive manager, Muriel had us singing musically and sensitively and also heartily from time to time. She teaches that what you believe should show through your music.'

Members of staff at today's music schools can be encouraged by what Bobby wrote:

'I have been a local officer in the Salvation Army for twenty-four years and still remember the leadership classes at these music schools: they included conducting techniques, music preparation, choice of music and working just within the ability of the group (but stretching them). Mostly however, I remember being told that being a music leader in the SA is 5% music and 95% people. Phrases such as 'friendly but not familiar – you may be called upon to make a difficult decision, you may become a confidante . . . Listen carefully'. These lessons have also been invaluable in my professional life.'

It seemed that Bobby arrived at that 1982 music school:

> 'With an overwhelming feeling that everybody else seemed to be so confident and to know so much about music – I was terrified that I would not be good enough to cope!'

Have you heard him sing recently?

An invitation to go to Sweden for their National Music School was quite a surprise, my first thought being, 'I can't speak Swedish'. Having been assured that this would not be a problem, I accepted. The dates were free, my husband was also invited, and as they wanted him to play E flat bass in the band, he was quite pleased to be involved. He was actually a euphonium player, but he borrowed an E flat bass and did some practising, only to find when we got there that he was required to play euphonium after all! All that E flat bass noise for nothing! Goran Larsson was the officer in charge of the music school; I was to share the girls' singing and to be totally responsible for the SATB work – something they had not done before – quite a challenge. At any music school, the choice of songs is vitally important. The 'big number' should be something to really challenge them but not so difficult that they cannot reach a high standard of performance. So I chose the songs with great care: *Jesus Thou art Everything to me* [words by E.H. Joy and A.S. Arnott, music by Len Ballantine], and *This Age of Rockets*. For the girls, *Joy because of You*, [words by Barbara Sampson, music by Trevor Davis] was a good choice – they loved it. The style of singing for these three songs was quite different from anything the students had previously attempted, but they seemed to enjoy thoroughly the English way of doing things.

Per Olsen was in charge of the bands – he was an enthusiast and something of a 'slave driver'; I believe that I was quite benign by comparison. My only problem that week, was on the Thursday: well-known in the Music School circles as the low point of the week. The final festival was to be on the evening of the following day – no time to waste. However 'Thursday lethargy' was setting in, and proving difficult to eradicate. My usual turn of phrase on such an occasion would not have the required impact on the Swedish-speaking group of young people. So I appealed to Gunnar:

'Can you "GIVE THEM A ROCKET"?'

'Sure thing.'

So I listened as he delivered some strong words in his own language – sensational! I never knew what he said or threatened: by just watching and listening I got the message – so did they! From then on, effort was redoubled and the conductor was a happy lady again. The final festival in Stockholm was really quite amazing: all these young people singing with fervent feelings in what was to them a foreign language.

About that time I went to Balvonie (the SA's lovely holiday and conference centre in Scotland) on two consecutive years to do the choral work at the Young People's leaders' conferences. Nothing gave me greater pleasure than helping and encouraging the leaders of our YP bands and singing companies. We had two sessions when everyone joined together to form a four-part choir. When the then territorial commander for Scotland, Commissioner Eva Burrows came to see us, we sang for her Joy Webb's *The Surprise*. She expressed surprise when she saw YP bandleaders non-reluctantly singing in the choir!

In the autumn of 1983 Hendon Songsters went to Plymouth Congress Hall for the weekend. The VIP guests were Colonels Brindley and Nina Boon and for the occasion we had been working on one of Brindley's many songster 'selections' - *Beautiful Zion*. Some pessimistic songsters had thought that the youngsters would not enjoy learning it, whereas in fact they sang it with conviction and pleasure. We do our young people, many of whom study music at school and college, a disservice if we do not include some of the Army's classics in the songster repertoire. I currently write to all new songster leaders, and always suggest to them that they should not neglect our choral music which has stood the test of time, music written by such people as George Marshall, Eric Ball, Charles Skinner and Ray Steadman-Allan, Brindley Boon and Ray Bowes.

On that Sunday morning at Plymouth we had a very long march from the open-air meeting to the Hall – I was exhausted, a feeling which stayed with me for the rest of the day. Following a lunchtime rehearsal, Brindley conducted his *Beautiful Zion* in the afternoon meeting. It was a great treat for us and a revelation to the younger members of the group. The long weekend finally came to an end, and the songsters went home by coach, whilst Bill and I stayed behind to spend two days with some friends. Now that the strain of the weekend was over, I should have felt better – but I didn't. A walk up a hill which left me breathless prompted my friend Marjorie Tilley (she had been my secretary at Northwood for many years) to insist that I see a doctor when I got home. This I did, which started off a train of events which led to my eventually having a quadruple heart by-pass in March 1984.

In the meantime, I continued as songster leader. In 1984 the Two-in-One Festival was held at the Guildhall in the City of London – I remember being extremely nervous as I conducted Hendon Songsters singing a selection of songs from Joy Webb's *Break Through*. The only other big events on the horizon were a Music Marathon in March and a weekend for the songsters at Bedlington. The Music Marathon was planned as a way of getting people into the Salvation Army hall and as a fundraiser. There was to be continuous music from 9 am to 9 pm, the last two hours of which would be the programme to be given at Bedlington a few weeks later. With my hospitalisation looming, and the prospect of heart surgery, I realised that it would be necessary for me to retire. A date was fixed for June, by which time it was expected that I would be fit to participate in a 'retirement' weekend. The songster locals were adamant that one should be arranged. My operation was to be the week before the Marathon. At a meeting of all the songster locals, we decided to ask Songster Leader Doug Collin of Staines Corps, if he could possibly take on the songsters for the three planned big events – the Marathon,

Bedlington weekend and my retirement. Doug and June were good friends; when at Northwood we had needed an adjudicator for a speech competition, Doug had spent the day with us. Amazingly, on this occasion, all these dates were free in his diary: the only problem was that the Staines Songster practice was on the same evening as Hendon – Thursday. With the co-operation of Steve Cobb, the Hendon bandmaster, the band and songsters swapped days and the problem was solved. 'The Lord Will Provide', is a text that readily comes to mind! We assured Doug, that his only responsibility would be the actual singing – everything else would be taken care of! Details of the arrangements for the Marathon I handed over to Malcolm Quinn; I knew that his was 'a safe pair of hands'.

I had no worries about the events that were imminent, and after my retirement in June my responsibility for the brigade would be over. There would be mixed feelings but I knew that the time was ripe for me to hand over to someone else. Plans for the weekend were in the hands of the songster local officers – all I had to do was to be there! Major John Mott was invited to be the guest speaker for the weekend, the Croydon Male Voice Quartet were booked for the Saturday evening festival and Songster Leader Doug Collin was preparing the songsters for that special weekend. I am reminded of a story in a book by John Jackson, whose regular Monday morning broadcasts in the 1970s had a huge listening public. He writes of the retirement of a railway stationmaster after fifty years at the same station. A great celebration was planned – a feed and a concert – all to be kept secret. On the day everything was in place but the 'Gaffer' didn't come – he'd gone out with his brother-in-law. It had all been so secret that no one had told him! Well my story is not quite like that, but at Hendon Salvation Army in June 1984 there was a big celebration for the years of service that the Songster Leader had given to that wonderful group of singers – everything was organized, all the people assembled at the Salvation Army Hall in Brampton Grove, but where was the 'Gaffer'? She wasn't there!

* * *

CHAPTER EIGHTEEN

'When we have exhausted our store of endurance,
our Father's full giving is only begun'.
(Annie J. Flint)

It should not have been a surprise to me that I had a serious heart problem. In 1943 my father had suddenly collapsed and died, as did my only sister in 1974. Two uncles and two cousins had also suffered the same fate, so as I prepared mentally for the bypass operation I was feeling extremely thankful that my problem had been diagnosed. On our way to the Princess Grace Hospital in the Harley Street area, a chance encounter uplifted my spirits. As my husband and I passed the Trinity College of Music we heard the strains of an orchestra.

'Let's go in. We are in good time.'

So in we went and sat as the only listeners to the orchestra as they rehearsed. It came as no surprise to me that Mark Bearcroft and Wallace Ruby were both there. Mark was involved with his electronic recording equipment, whilst Wallace was doing percussion work with the orchestra. (Wallace and I had worked together for him to get his Grade 8 singing). When there was a break they both came to speak to us – just the tonic I needed!

On that Thursday I was installed in the hospital and my consultant surgeon – Mr Alun Rees – came in to see me.

'Saturday is the day. It will be 'ladies first' – 8 am for you. I'll be very careful: we don't want too many scars, do we?'

When on the Saturday he came to see me after the operation, he was very pleased with the result:

'I did four bypasses, just to be on the safe side.'

Eight days later I was home with instructions to do nothing – not even make a cup of tea – for the next two weeks. Help was needed. A family member – Freda – offered to use two weeks of annual leave to look after me. Short walks, gradually increasing in length were also prescribed for the near future. Visits from my local GP and good care at home contributed much to a trouble-free recovery.

My retirement weekend was fast approaching – I wondered if I would be able to conduct just one song. Mr Rees, whom I was seeing regularly, would have to be consulted.

'Go ahead. You'll be all right. You have made a remarkable recovery.'

At the same time I asked him about a proposed visit to Australia at the beginning of 1985. Commissioner Eva Burrows had invited me to do some choral training and conducting – it was to be a very busy programme. Again he gave me a 'no problems' answer. So I went to a songster practice – it was arranged that on the pre-retirement Sunday morning I would conduct just one song – *God's World*, [words M. Burton, music T. Parry] - and if it went well, I would do the same on my retirement Sunday. I knew the song, as did the Songsters: they were familiar and comfortable with it: all would be well.

But when Sunday morning came, all was not well. As we were starting to sing the second verse and after saying to them: 'Carry on singing.' I sank to the floor. Apparently they did carry on singing: two more verses, then back to verse one – and so on.

Catherine Renshaw, a highly-qualified nurse, and Blair Allan a medical student from America, cared for me until the ambulance arrived. I do remember Blair saying to me,

'Muriel, can you see me?'

'How can I see you when my eyes are closed?'

Those were possibly the last words I spoke until a week the following Thursday when I finally regained consciousness. It was a long time before I realised what had happened – after a week in a coma and on the Sunday evening of my actual retirement weekend, I had a life-saving brain operation performed by a world-renowned surgeon who was prepared to have his Sunday disturbed! In the afternoon of that near-fatal Sunday, Major John

Mott apparently came to the hospital to see me and gave me the Salvation Army equivalent of 'the last rites'. He has since told me that he did not expect to see me again. I remember gaining consciousness and being surprised that I was in hospital and totally unable to move. Soon the questions from the nursing staff began:

'Mrs Yendell, do you know what day it is?'

'No. But if you tell me what day it was yesterday, I think I'll be able to tell you what day it is today.'

'Mrs Yendell, can you tell me the name of the Prime Minister?'

'It's Mrs Thingumpty.'

And so on.

'Do you know what hospital you are in?'

'No idea.'

I was in Maida Vale hospital which was scheduled for closure in the near future: as my brain began to function I sensed that there was a feeling of hopelessness about the place – at least in the wards. The clinical care was brilliant, and I owe my life to that and to the surgeon. When he was happy with my progress, I was moved to Edgware Hospital. Before I left, I was told that they were keeping the bone which had been removed from my head:

'Just in case we have to go in again!'

I shuddered at the thought. If all went well, I would return to Maida Vale in September to have the bone re-inserted.

'In the meantime, take care not to bump your head.'

Edgware Hospital was to be my home for the next six weeks. The nursing staff were fantastic, and they soon had me out of bed into a chair, after which I insisted on sitting out for all my meals. My first real treat was when they wheeled me in a special 'contraption' to the bathroom and lowered me into the lovely hot water. It was heaven! I thought they would wash my hair! But they couldn't – there was no hair to wash! Until that point I had not realised that my head had been shaved. When I got back to my bed I used the window as a mirror – what a sight! It really was most upsetting. However, common sense prevailed and I set about thinking what I could do about it. When my husband came to see me, he was given strict instructions where to find my small headscarves – please would he bring them to the hospital immediately!

These headscarves came to be worn at all visiting times: no one was expected at any other times, so 'headscarves after lunch' was the order of the day. However, one morning, I saw a man in Salvation Army uniform walking towards me down the centre of the ward: he was carrying a large bunch of roses. At that moment I happened to be listening to some music on my portable head-set. The man came straight to me, and his opening words were,

> 'You must be the only skin-head songster leader in the business.'

Yes, it was my good friend Norman Bearcroft (Colonel) with whom I had been involved in so much SA music-making.

One night a drunken youth barged into the ward – that was quite exciting. Then a neighbouring patient put her false teeth in my glass of water, and another was found to be wearing my bed-jacket. But the best of all was when Hendon Band came to play to us. Mostly they stayed outside, but several of them came into the ward. (I had been in the habit of joining the band for hospital visitation – now I was on the receiving end). My fellow patients thought that they had merely come to see me, since I was a Salvationist.

'Not so,' I explained. Those Sunday morning visits were the highlight of the week. When I was being discharged, the ladies asked me,

> 'Will the band come, now that you are leaving?'

> 'Oh yes! They'll be here'.

It was quite a proud moment for me.

Learning to walk again was both a pleasure and a chore. At first, I was propped up between two nurses; then I was given a 'Zimmer' frame, followed by one on wheels, which tended to run away from me. Finally, a walking stick was all I needed. One day I heard the consultant say to the staff nurse:

'When this lady can walk down and up the stairs
(just outside the ward) we will let her go home.'

From then on the stairs were my target and gradually I was able to do as required. The day came for my discharge. My belongings were gathered up, my stick given to me, and I was ready to walk out – not before I had given my stick to my husband.

'I'm walking out of here on my own two feet.'

The first Saturday I was home, Jim and Jean Wilson had invited us to spend the afternoon with them in their garden and stay to tea – it was my first social outing since that fateful Sunday. Just before we left home, a huge bouquet of flowers was delivered, with a message from the Territorial Music School 1984 – I should have been there! The pleasure and encouragement it gave me cannot be over-estimated. When we arrived at Jim's home, I asked him,

'Is there any way we can contact the music school
at the Fairfield Halls?'

'Yes, I'll fix that. What message do you want me
to give?'

'Just say how thrilled I was to receive their
bouquet of flowers, and that I immediately began
to feel better. Sorry to miss them.'

It wasn't long before Jim came back into the room with a 'mission accomplished' broad smile.

Whilst I had been in hospital, my husband had been looking for a smaller house: he already had a buyer for our property, but had not found a suitable alternative. Although I tried hard to go with him to view properties, it was all too exhausting – even traumatic. There was an obvious solution to our problem: decamp to the Bognor Regis flat. This we did, taking with us the necessities and putting everything else in store. Our friends Ray and Maisie Wiggins helped Bill to deal with this: I was safely ensconced in our lovely flat overlooking the sea, having been carried up the forty-three steps to our flat door, courtesy St. John's Ambulance. This was the point at which it became obvious that the spur-of-the-moment purchase of the flat, was meant to be – it had not been a matter of chance. My personal belief is that without direct intervention, God sometimes puts ideas into our minds and leaves the decisions to us. Was it by chance that in 1980 I had said to Bill, as we passed an estate agent's window,

'Let's go in and ask if he has any 'sea-view' flats for sale'.

He had two – one with an 'oblique' view of the sea, and the other was the flat with which we fell in love. For me, it was the ideal place to recuperate. After two weeks I risked going out for a short walk on the promenade, having persuaded myself that the stairs would not prove insurmountable on my return. Each day a longer walk was possible, until I reached my goal – to walk to Felpham! Then I moved the goal-posts! Felpham and back would soon be attempted. My strength was returning, but there was still a big problem to be solved.

What about my hair? It was growing very slowly but 'coming on nicely' when I received a summons to go to the still-functioning Maida Vale Hospital for the replacement of my bone. By that time the hospital was even nearer its own demise and things had only got worse. Although there was a No Smoking notice in the four-bed ward, two of the patients smoked inveterately. The nurse said that as they were both terminally ill, there was nothing she could do. At one point I did manage to persuade the ladies to use the 'smoking room' but this they did only occasionally. I was admitted on a Monday morning – by 10.30 am was the instruction. Once I was in the ward, I was told that due to a very big 'technical hitch' I might not be able to have the operation the next day: I could stay, or leave. My choice was to stay and hope for the best. Not until evening did anyone come to see me. A harassed and obviously exhausted young doctor came and did the obligatory tests. If I was prepared to be optimistic about what would happen on the morrow, I would have to fast.

'I'll fast', was my retort.

As he was leaving me, the young man said,

'I expect they'll take the bone out of your hip.'

My immediate horrified reaction was to call out, 'Come back here, young man.'

I think he was a bit startled.

'Nobody is taking any bone out of my hip and I am NOT walking out of here on crutches!'

He was perplexed, he was speechless.

'You've got my bone here somewhere, just go and find it!'

Off he went obviously somewhat troubled. Soon a nursing sister arrived at my bedside.

'Don't worry Mrs Yendell. They are looking for your bone. If they can't find it, they'll make you one.'

Nothing more to be done: no food to be eaten, and I had to wait anxiously whilst they searched for my bone. In the morning the operation was on: the sister came to tell me they had found my bone – 'It was in the dustbin!' That was her little joke: it had actually been stored in a 'fridge'.

Another strange thing happened as I was lying on the trolley waiting for the 'jab'. I was shown a letter from a Mr Gareth Rees, a heart surgeon at a hospital unknown to me. In it he wrote that he was pleased to have received such a good report about me.

'I don't know a Mr Gareth Rees. My surgeon was a Mr Alun Rees.'

'Oh no: it was Gareth Rees: this is his letter with his signature.'

Since I was lying flat on my back, waiting for the 'jab' I was hardly in a position to argue. I left it at that, and asked please would they remove as little hair as possible from my head. The anaesthetist promised they would do their best.

When Bill came to see me that evening, I told him the story of the letter. He investigated the matter and discovered that Edgware Hospital had reported my case to the wrong Mr Rees, and that my surgeon – Mr Alun Rees, had no idea what had happened to me. That mistake could have had serious consequences. After a week in hospital, the stitches in my head were removed by a very nervous young nurse.

'It's the first time I've done this!'

'Don't worry – you're doing well.'

And finally, I discovered that all my toiletries and make-up had been stolen from the bedside cabinet. That week was quite an experience.

It was a great relief to be taken home to Bognor – the beautiful fresh sea air was a tonic to me and once again I resumed my sea-front walks. As we were now permanently in the flat, we started to go to Bognor Regis Salvation Army – just the morning meeting, and no uniform for me – a Salvation Army bonnet was hardly compatible with a half-bald head.

For the first time in my life I started to go to the Home-League and I have been a Home-Leaguer ever since. The Monday afternoon meetings gave me a chance to get to know a few people: they were very friendly to this strange, thin, pale lady who always wore a head scarf. It was to be months before my hair got back to normal. A retired Major often sat next to me at the Monday afternoon meetings. One day we had a conversation – a question and answer session!

'What did you say your name is?'

'Muriel.'

'Yes, I know. But Muriel what?'

'Muriel Yendell.'

She scrutinized my face closely, and then said, 'Are you THE Muriel Yendell?'

Somewhat embarrassed, I replied,

'If you mean what I think you mean, yes I am.'

She had worked for many years in the youth department at NHQ and because of my heavy involvement with music schools and leaders conferences she had recognized the name. It was at this point in my life that I became involved with the home-league singers. The Commanding Officer at Bognor, Ann Wilmot, was herself a good pianist and composer. One day she asked me if I could play the piano. My affirmative answer caused her to give me some copies of songs the home-league singers were currently using, and expressed the hope that the music would not be too difficult for me. It was a small group of keen and competent singers. When she was moved from Bognor, I became their leader for the next three years – my rehabilitation had begun.

My next big step towards normality was when Captain Dianne Lillicrap (now Colonel D. O'Brien) invited me to go to the Bristol Divisional Music School for two days as a guest. She assured me that I would not have to do any work. Her other guest was Peter Graham, whom I was very pleased to meet. All I was expected to do was spend some time with the girls in rehearsal and, if I felt up to it, to do some teaching. One of the songs was *Joy because of You*, [words Barbara Sampson, music, Trevor Davis] with which I was very familiar. So, not feeling too confident, I did some teaching and discovered that I was not as hopeless as might be expected. That song became my song, but conducting it in the church on the Wednesday evening was out-of-the-question. At the last rehearsal before the mid-week concert, Dianne told me that they wanted me to conduct them.

'That's nice of you, but no, I don't think I can do it: it would be too nerve-wracking.'

'We will help you,' was the choir's response.

That was so moving: I could no longer refuse. Details of that occasion are permanently etched on my memory. The very high pulpit was the conductor's rostrum. Even climbing up the steps to it was something of a challenge. I just simply planted my feet firmly on the floor of the pulpit and stood as if glued to the spot for the whole song: three verses, three choruses and a coda. The normal situation in which a choral director works was completely turned upside-down. It is my belief that in performance, the conductor must inspire the choir to sing better than they have ever done. At that church, it was the singers who did the inspiring – they enabled me to get through a frightening experience and thus kick-started my musical journey back on the road to normality.

Thanks to Dianne for the invitation, and to the girls of the Bristol Division for their confidence in me, and their encouragement. In that church, *Joy because of You*, became a very special song for me.

* * *

CHAPTER NINETEEN
'To God be the Glory, great things He has done'.
(Fanny Crosby)

In writing this last chapter, which is also the last chapter of my life, I have so much for which to be thankful. My twenty-one years since the miracle of the life-saving brain operation on the Sunday evening of my 'retirement' weekend have been full of opportunities to use not only whatever talents I have, but also, and perhaps more importantly, to use my experience to help and encourage others. Perhaps 'miracle' is too strong a word to use in connection with my survival: it was retired Commissioner Mrs Holbrook who first used it to describe my complete recovery.

At some point during my stay at Harefield Hospital, the matron's name was mentioned, 'Miss Holbrook'. My enquiries confirmed that she was the daughter of Commissioner Holbrook. A nurse agreed to point her out to me when she came into the ward. It was not long before a very smart lady approached my bed:

'Mrs Yendell, were you asking for me?'

'Well, if you are Miss Holbrook, the answer is "Yes".'

We had a lovely chat; she seemed pleased that I knew her Salvation Army parents. After she left, my status as a patient had improved – the matron had paid a social visit!

Some time later at Sunbury Court at a songster leaders' refresher course (very refreshing) Mrs Commissioner Holbrook came as a guest speaker. This sort of encounter has happened so often over the years that the word 'co-incidence' is no longer in my vocabulary. Noman Bearcroft introduced me to our guest. Lifting both hands in the air, she exclaimed loudly,

'Oh! You are the miracle!'

Everybody heard her – it was stunning. She explained to all present that she hosted a prayer group at her home and that all of them had been praying for me.

In one of her books, Flora Larsson wrote,

> 'I believe that when we pray for people, we help to create a climate of goodwill and love around them which God can use for their benefit.'

The book, *Christus Victor* written by Dennis and Pauline Hunter, contains these words:

> 'Purposeful intercession flowing along wavebands of forceful spiritual energy creates its own mysterious power'.

The truth of these words has been proved in my own life. Spiritual and physical strength has been received through prayers offered on my behalf.

My four years at Bognor Regis Corps were very happy ones: a full recovery meant that after a medical examination, my driving licence was returned to me, and along with it, my independence. There were miles of promenade. When I was finally able to walk from home to Felpham and back, it seemed that my recovery was complete.

Becoming involved again in choral music was a real bonus. Home League singers are generally regarded as the very poor relations of songster brigades, but both at Bognor and at Staines they were not only keen to sing well but capable of producing some very good results. The size of a group is of very little consequence: after all, the famous Kings Singers are only five in number! Commitment, willingness to learn and a desire to do the best of which they are capable ensure that the finished product will be worth hearing.

As ever with my enterprises things begin to proliferate and the singing group increased in size. Major Millicent Straker arrived at the corps and immediately was involved in the home league, eventually becoming the home league secretary. She was an enthusiastic member of the home league singers and became, and still remains a personal friend who later proved to be my proverbial 'friend in time of need'.

We produced a Christmas Worship at the Home League, then an Easter worship. We visited residential homes and local churches and had our own Home League weekend at the corps. For all this I was not only the leader for the group, but also the pianist – which had some advantages. I've always felt that no pianist is better that any pianist! The accompaniment tapes available at SP&S are wonderful for groups who just simply do not have anyone to play the piano but it seemed to me that a pre-set speed and lack of flexibility would be very restrictive. However, it suddenly dawned on me that the piano accompaniment could be recorded by me – surely that would be satisfactory! But it wasn't! The speed on the tape was my speed, and yet it was totally inflexible as if the music were set in concrete! One performance of that was enough. When we were invited to sing at a divisional meeting – quite an accolade – it was back to the piano for me and an unconducted performance from the singers. If the singers are comfortable with their song and know it so well that it is safe, then singing without a conductor can often have an immediate and effective impact on the listeners – direct communication.

Whilst at Bognor I was often invited to Portsmouth Citadel to do some work with the songsters at their Thursday evening rehearsal. It was immensely enjoyable: no responsibilities, no forward planning – just doing my favourite thing again against all expectations. John Bird, the songster leader, was doing me a good turn. Gradually I began to get involved again in Salvation Army music-making: music schools, songster weekends and rehearsals. In 1991 the first adult music school was held at Butlin's Holiday Camp, Skegness with Howard Evans in charge and Colonel Ray Steadman-Allen and me as his assistants, we had a very good team. Two top-class pianists on the staff meant that the choice of songs was not limited by the ability of the accompanists! On the Friday we were timetabled to present a programme to two audiences: this was a great motivator. Several male 'students' had opted for the choral group – we rehearsed at the same time as the band in which several ladies played: the notion that only men play instruments and ladies sing was shattered. At one point in the daily programme the whole group joined together for massed singing, and I was able to use Kevin Norbury's *Rejoicings* one year, and Peter Graham's *Paean* the next. After the second year, the school was dropped from the Territorial Music Calendar, and was restarted at Sunbury Court with a shortened week (Monday to Friday) and no final festival. It has, nevertheless, continued to flourish and because of the venue has become a great social as well as a spiritual and musical occasion. That it is generally oversubscribed bears witness to its popularity.

In the autumn of 1984, Hendon Songsters invited Bill and me to a 'retirement dinner' to be held at the RAF Museum in Hendon. This was totally unexpected but much appreciated – a very special occasion. A photograph of the event reveals that although not yet having a 'good head of hair', my hairstyle was passable, thanks to an innovative hairdresser in Bognor! Making a speech was not easy; after twenty-one years at Hendon, there was a strong emotional attachment. So it was kept as light as possible, with a passing reference to my hole-in-the-head situation! For me it was a momentous event.

It was whilst at Bognor that it became obvious to me that I had a hearing problem. Taking the necessary steps to deal with it meant a visit to the GP, then to the clinic and finally to see a specialist at the local hospital. No test results had been given to me by then, so I did not know what to expect. In the consultant's room, a man was sitting at his desk, busy writing. Without looking at me he said something about hearing aids.

'Oh, are you going to give me hearing-aids?'

Still not looking up from his papers he rather brusquely said,

'No, I'm not. It is not my job. It's the technician's job.'

Equally brusquely I replied,

'Then I'll rephrase the question. Am I to be given hearing aids?'

At this point he looked at me, realised that he was speaking to a human being and from that point on, he tried to be quite pleasant. I didn't make it easy for him. Since then, over the years, my hearing has deteriorated. Thankfully, my latest hearing aids, with a special 'music' facility, are the best so far – certainly there is more pleasure in listening to music. Unfortunately they seem to be allergic to Salvation Army bands!

In 1988 we were living very happily at Bognor Regis in our lovely home overlooking the sea, revelling in the gorgeous sea-air and the beautiful surrounding countryside. A big bonus was that family and friends often visited us – a lovely place for a holiday. Then near-disaster struck again! Our neighbour, Tony John, had died. We had gone to his funeral at the Roman Catholic Church to which he and his family belonged. Should we wear our Salvation Army Uniform? 'Yes' was our immediate decision. We put the use of our flat at the disposal of the large John family, many of whom said how pleased they were to see us in our Salvation Army uniform in the church. There was to be a memorial service at the Actor's Church in London – Tony had been a significant theatre director and was much involved in his training scheme for young thespians. So we, with our other next-door neighbours, John and Jenny, caught the London train. Before we reached the first stop, Bill collapsed. As we pulled into Pulborough station, a porter was called. Everything happened very quickly: a wheel chair was brought, John organised the calling of an ambulance, and soon we were on our way to Chichester Hospital. Jenny was the only one to continue the journey to London. After two weeks Bill came home: now it was his turn to find the forty plus steps to our flat door a problem. It seemed to me that we would need to move again and we began to look for somewhere suitable in Bognor. My own preference was for moving back into the London area where our families lived, and this is what we eventually decided to do.

We found a very pleasant and suitable house in Chertsey, said our farewells to Bognor, and arranged for our goods, plus those still in storage, to be taken to our new home – at last I would have my piano back! Having made sure that all legal and financial matters had been dealt with, we set out at the same time as the removal van – we would be in our new home by the end of the day! What happened next was unbelievable! The vendors said that they had not received confirmation that the payment had been received, therefore they would not be handing over the keys! So we waited and waited and waited. Our next door neighbours-to-be allowed us to use their telephone (no mobile phones) to try and get confirmation that the monies really had been sent to the vendor's solicitor. The removal men were getting fidgety and eventually they left, to return early the next day.

In the early evening, having been assured that the deposit had been paid, the vendors gave us the keys and left. That night I stayed with my son Andrew, in his home at Sunbury Court, and Bill, liberally supplied with food, blankets, pillows and a radio, slept on the floor in number 15 Canford Drive. The next day we waited for the removal van and from that point on, all went according to plan. The home and the garden were in pristine condition; that was a bonus we felt we deserved in view of the removal firm's somewhat extortionate charge for the overnight delay in delivering and unloading our goods and chattels.

My son Andrew and his family - wife Else-Anne, daughter Marianne and son Michael - were all at Staines Corps, so that is where we decided to worship. The first time I went to the home league, they were having a garden party. We did not know many people at Staines, and I had no idea who was in the home league. But the Salvation Army magic was at work again. As I went into the garden, someone called out,

'Hello Muriel.'

Some years previously we had been on holiday in Malta, staying at the Salvation Army Red Shield Club. John and Jean Denyer had also been there and it was Jean who had called out to me. When you have been a Salvationist for many years, in my case life-long, I believe it to be almost impossible to go into any Salvation Army community without there being a connection to someone there:

'Oh, you come from Staines. Do you know Doug and June Collin?'

Not surprisingly. I was soon involved in some music-making. Kath Thornhill, the fairly newly appointed home league secretary, was planning to do a home league Christmas carol service, a new venture. Would I be prepared to get together a group of singers to take part in the carol service? It was too much of a temptation – I was hooked.

We asked for volunteers – no auditions – and about sixteen ladies made up the group. Both Kath and Jean were excellent sopranos and there were a few good altos of whom Major Margaret Davis was one. With her husband Trevor she was stationed at Staines Corps.

The choice of songs was crucial, as it nearly always is. Easy but effective was the criterion. Joy Webb's *A Starry Night* (unison) and a lovely two-part song *A Night Divine* [words and music by John Wells] – two contrasting songs – proved to be just what we needed. June Collin would be available on the day – just one quick run through with her before the carol service was the finishing touch we needed. Major Trevor Davis heard this rehearsal – would we sing at the Sunday evening corps carol service? I wasn't sure about that. Staines Songsters and Singing Company would also be taking part – although it was not a competition, we would not be happy to be the poor relations! I was never a risk-taker when it came to performing in public; it would not necessarily be 'all right on the night'. But it was all right on the Tuesday so, yes we would be pleased to be part of the corps carol service. The not very big hall was packed out – no place for the home league singers to sit together. I sat with my family. Andrew asked, rather apprehensively,

'Are they going to do all right, mum?'

'Wait and see.'

I thought the answer should have been 'Yes', but I too was waiting to see!

For the Joy Webb song, I had persuaded Dave Cooper (although he did not need much persuading) to give us a bass fiddle accompaniment: it worked really well. The debut of what was to become the home league singers was a huge success. Not surprisingly the singers wanted to keep the group going, and thus was the Staines Home League Singers formed. Eventually June Collin was available on Tuesday afternoons – what a difference that made! We developed a busy programme, visiting several other home league meetings and one Saturday evening we actually did a whole programme – with the help of a young horn player, Susan Betts, and a violinist, Sarah Wilson.

Our biggest undertaking was a musical *The White Rose*, written by John Larsson for Home League singers - with the help of Ceinwen Gardiner in the star role. Doug Collin produced it, giving the needed professional touch. At a much earlier date, he had visited Northwood School. As an English/Drama adviser in a neighbouring borough, he was the ideal man to adjudicate speech competitions. The musical was performed again at the next divisional home league rally.

By the time the new Salvation Army hall was opened in 1996, the Home League singers had become part of the Staines Corps scene, singing at the opening 'festival' Howard Davies' *How can I Thank You?* Soon afterwards, a Tuesday afternoon men's fellowship was launched. The Leader, Wesley Maughan, suggested we try to form a mixed singing group – it seemed the logical next step. So the fellowship singers came into being. I did the initial work with them but realized that I really should retire. By this time June Collin, having retired from teaching was doing the accompaniments and Doug Collin was singing in the group. A change was made; Doug took on the fellowship singers with June at the piano, then June took over the home league singers whilst I did the piano work. (I always thought that Doug was fortunate that wherever he went as a songster leader/musical director, he took his own brilliant pianist with him!)

Then Doug decided to move house. At one time when they were agonizing about which of two houses to buy, June rang to ask if she could come to see me. She needed someone with whom she could discuss a dilemma. The choice was between a house close enough to Staines for them to still come to the corps, and another one in Bedfordshire which would take them away from Staines but would be nearer their daughter who often needed their help. What should they do? We talked it over, the pros and cons of each house. This seemed to help June, not to come to a decision, but to clarify things in her own mind. Before she left, I said,

'Would you like a promise from my 'Promise Box'?'

'Yes please,' she replied.

So she took one out, read it silently and then started to laugh! What could be funny about that, I wondered.

'Listen to this Muriel:

'I the Lord thy God will be with thee whithersoever thou goest'.'

Nothing could have been more appropriate than that. It didn't matter what they decided: they had the promise which is given to all believers, the truth of which I had experienced for myself over and over again. They chose the house near their daughter, which has proved to be the right choice. Meanwhile, Wes Maughan and I, with the help of Christine Thomas kept the singing groups going until Ann Fuller came along.

Ann, together with her husband Fred and mother, Colonel Mrs Drury, had moved to Staines Corps from Guildford. It was quite a while before I knew that Ann was a well-qualified and experienced music teacher, and had a very good track record as a choral conductor. 'The Lord will provide' seemed an appropriate text. Using a 'softly, softly' approach we gradually caught her interest. Ann came along to a rehearsal and she was hooked. 'Hallelujah'. Ann is a superb choral teacher, and under her direction, the fellowship and home league singers continue to thrive.

In 1996, after months of deteriorating health, my husband Bill was 'Promoted to Glory'. He had been a Salvationist all his life. A recent regret had been that he had not been fit enough to go to his grand-daughter's wedding in New Zealand. So I thought it would be a good thing for me to visit Alison and Jason in Wellington and arranged to go in 1997. It would also give me a chance to see my old friend Commissioner Marjorie Goffin.

It suddenly occurred to me that rather than doing a return trip to Wellington, a round-the-world ticket would allow me to return home via Los Angeles. So here the Salvation Army 'Mafia' came into its own. Lots of letters were written, calendars consulted and an itinerary created, all of which was booked with British Airways by my daughter-in-law Else-Anne:

Heathrow to Cape Town: Friday to Monday.

With Colin Morley, a former Songster at Hendon.

Cape Town to Perth: Monday to Friday. With Jacqui Proctor – former National Songster and a good friend.

Perth to Sydney: Friday to Monday. With Margaret Ross who had stayed with us when the Sydney Staff Songsters visited Staines.

Sydney to Brisbane: Monday to Friday. With Edna and Allan Nutter and Irene Johnson all of whom were in the Songsters at Nelson in the 1940s.

Brisbane to Wellington: Friday to Thursday. To stay with the newly-weds.

Wellington to Sydney: Thursday to Friday. (I went back to Sydney so as not to have to spend two nights on my own in Fiji.)

Sydney to Los Angeles: Friday to Monday. With Ivor and Jeanette Bosanko.

Los Angeles to Heathrow: Monday.

As I had walked through the 'gate' at Heathrow, waving to Else-Anne and Marianne, I thought,

'What have I done? What am I doing here? I must be mad'.

But once on the plane, I had settled down to enjoy the most wonderful holiday – everything went according to plan; there were some incredible experiences. Outstanding was the Sunday evening meeting at Sydney Congress Hall led by Majors Derek and Helen Tyrrel, and featuring a group of ladies from a nearby Salvation Army social home. They sang to us with great devotion. A bonus for me was that my friends Commissioners Keith and Pauline Banks were sitting next to me - they had conducted the morning meeting. I had not seen them for a long time, but we had kept in touch. This world-wide Salvation Army to which I belong is itself a miracle!

1998 heralded the 50th Anniversary of the first 'music camp' for girls at Sunbury Court: in 1997 there had been a band reunion to celebrate the 1947 'band camp' - why not a 'singers' reunion? Enquiries revealed that THQ had no plans for such an event, so I took it on myself with the help of Malcolm and Kim Quinn and their friends Alan and Janice Beal. Sunbury Court was booked for a long weekend, Staines Corps readily co-operated – they provided a superb Sunday tea for the delegates and families/friends, and allowed us to conduct the evening meeting. A lot of work was involved but it all came together. I wanted us to have something special to sing; we needed a Gowans/Bosanko song. The result of my requests to each of these two outstanding writers is the song *The Stones Cry Out*. It is highly unlikely that many people have heard or sung the entire work, but a prayer in it has gone round the world:

In this quiet moment, still before Your throne,
Conscious of Your presence, knowing I am known,
In this quiet moment set my singing free.
In this quiet moment, make a better me!

I had invited Jeanette Bosanko to teach and conduct her husband's composition; it was a *tour de force*. After the meeting I said to her,

> 'Asking you to teach and conduct *The Stones Cry Out* was the biggest sacrifice I have ever made.'

To which she replied,

> 'I'm glad you made it!'

In November of that year a 'retirement' meeting was held for me at the Staines Corps. Captain Peter Ayling was the territorial headquarters representative, and I was presented with a framed certificate 'In recognition of exceptional service'. The text at the bottom of the certificate is

> 'Inasmuch as ye have done it unto the least of these my brethren, ye have done it unto Me' (Matthew 25:40).

The only thing that I have done is develop whatever talents the Lord gave me, and used them in His service in the Salvation Army. Whatever I have been asked to do, I have done it, if it were possible. I gave it 'my best shot!' It has always been my joy to help and encourage young people to use and develop their talents – a talent is a gift.

Recently, in conversation with Kevin Ashman (Staff Band principal solo cornet player and songster leader at Maidstone) he spoke to me of the Manchester Music School where we met.

> 'Could you put that in writing?' I asked.

> 'Yes, sure – glad to.'

Here is what he wrote:

'I have always enjoyed attending the Salvation Army's Music Schools, both as a student and staff member. I remember one particular year when I was on the staff of the Manchester Division School with Muriel Yendell. I was heading up the brass side and she the vocal. As a young and inexperienced leader, it was a great delight to share the leadership of the school with Muriel – with all her years of experience.

'She spoke to me in the staff room one evening and suggested that it might be a good idea if I conducted one of the 'whole school' vocal items.

'"It would give the singing more credibility with the band lads if you did some singing with them".

'I was certainly not going to argue with Muriel's experienced opinion, so agreed to conduct Jane Clark and Len Ballantine's setting of *Jesus Thou Art Everything to Me* - I enjoyed the experience immensely. She was ready with observations that gave me confidence and helped me shape the music. It was a very rewarding experience for me – and one that helped me decide to accept the position of songster leader at Maidstone Corps when it was offered to me some ten years ago. Sure, I love my banding, but I also have a deep love for vocal music and enjoy the privilege of leading Maidstone Songster Brigade.

'My thanks to you, Muriel, for that first opportunity!'

On the 17th January 2001, a letter I received, prompted me to ring my son Andrew immediately.

'I've had a letter from Buckingham Palace!'

'What?'

'Yes, Buckingham Palace.'

'What's it about?'

'I've been nominated for Maundy Money.'

I could not believe it! Who could have nominated me? Perhaps there was some mistake. A telephone call to a given number assured me that there was no mistake. From then on, I was in a bit of a flutter of excitement. The first thought that comes to us ladies is 'What shall I wear?' Would wearing my Salvation Army uniform look out of place; would it make me too conspicuous? What was the alternative? Could I justify spending a large sum of money on an outfit for which there would be no further use?

None of these questions should have arisen, because I knew what ought to be done – my Salvation Army uniform it had to be. When I arrived at Westminster Abbey several other Salvationists were conspicuous. Later, I discovered that the Salvation Army had been asked for a number of nominations, and Colonel Trevor Davis, the Divisional Commander of our Division, had done me the honour. This was a big occasion when I didn't need a new outfit, just a professional cleaning for my uniform and a visit to the hairdressers – complete with my Salvation Army hat!

'This is what I shall be wearing tomorrow: do your best!'

Trevor Davis had thoughtfully asked for an extra ticket for my guests, so that my daughter-in-law, Else-Anne, and both my grandchildren, Michael and Marianne, could be admitted to the Abbey.

On entering the Nave, I hesitated long enough to locate my family in the congregation, then took my seat – Andrew, my 'companion' was immediately behind me. The pageantry and the music were magnificent – unforgettable. We were seated in alphabetical order which meant that I would be the last person to receive the bag of specially minted coins 'Thank you Your Majesty' or 'Thank you ma'am' were the permitted expressions of thanks to be accompanied by a curtsy or a 'bob'. I chose the latter – much easier than a curtsy; my response was the shorter of the two alternatives.

I am a collector of quotations, even supplying Staines Corps with its 'pause for thought' which appears each week in the Corps newsletter *Cupola*. My most recent find suits me very well at this time of my life:

> 'The shell grows old, but not the inhabited intellect'.

For me, life is only as busy as I like to make it. My music is limited to being a reserve pianist and also reserve conductor for the fellowship chorus and the home league singers at Staines. Occasionally I help out with some teaching of the aural work in Associated Board Music exams as well as accompanying instrumentalists at the actual examination – this at the request of my friend Maisie Wiggins. Recently, I had the pleasure of being her piano accompanist when she gave a short recital at Feltham Corps.

Having been involved in teaching since 1941, encouraging young people (and some not so young) to develop the talents which have been given to them is the most important contribution I can make in my continuing service as a 'Christian Soldier'. People sometimes say to me,

> 'You encouraged me.'

If any reward is needed, those three words are it.

The prayer of Sir Francis Drake, which was one of my favourite readings for school assembly, is most appropriate for all of us:

> 'O Lord God, when thou givest to Thy servants to endeavour any great matter, grant us also to know that it is not the beginning but the continuing of the same until it is thoroughly finished which yieldeth the true glory'.

* * *

LASTING JOYS – EPILOGUE

September 2003

A young man was standing in the foyer of the Staines Salvation Army Hall – Bandsman Paul Dymott. With no-one else about as I left the worship hall I went to speak to him.

'Hello Paul; it's unusual to see you here on a Tuesday afternoon,' (home league meeting).

'I've just been for an interview for post-graduate teacher training.'

'Very interesting. How did you get on?'

'Fine; I've been accepted. The man who interviewed me knows you.'

'Oh! Tell me more.'

'At one point in the interview I told him that I am a Salvationist.' (Full marks to Paul.) 'Then he said that he once worked in a comprehensive school where the head teacher was a Salvationist.'

Knowing that Paul had just got his mathematics degree, I immediately knew who the Interviewer must be.

'Was that a Mr Vertes?'

'Yes.'

'That's Bob Vertes – he was head of maths at Northwood.'

Thus has my story come full circle.

* * *

POSTSCRIPT

On a visit to Ivor and Jeanette Bosanko in April 2002, I asked Ivor if he would write a four-part song for Staines Corps 'Fellowship Chorus'. Handing me a song book, he said,

'Choose something.'

I opened the book at random – and there at number 600 was *Jesus Thou Art Everything to Me*. It was 'made to measure'; the song had to be fairly simple, some unison for both male and female voices, something for the men on their own and a not-too-difficult piano accompaniment. We love it: and now in this book it is being made available for all to enjoy and be moved by it.

●   *   *

For Muriel

Lasting Joys

Edward Joy (verses)
Conductor Score
Arthur Arnott (chorus)

Ivor Bosanko

Ivor Bosanko composing
'Lasting Joys'

ABOUT THE AUTHOR

MURIEL YENDELL was a product of the early 1920s spending her early years in Nelson, Lancashire, participating in the Whitefield School choir in its musical competitions, and progressing at the outbreak of World War II to a college in Sheffield from which she graduated as a teacher. Subsequent teaching appointments took her to Bradley School, Nelson, where she successfully undertook a course with the Royal Academy of Music, south to Toddington near Luton in Bedfordshire, to Vincent School in Northolt, then on to the Manor School at Ruislip as Senior Mistress, before promotion occurred in her appointment as deputy Head Teacher at Northwood School, where she was later to emerge as the school's Head Teacher.

In her other role as a convinced and active Salvationist she was involved with youth work at Nelson before being appointed in 1945 as the corps Songster Leader. In 1950 she moved to Luton, and then on to Harrow where once more she became the corps Songster Leader. In the years that followed she was to become Director of Music at various Summer Music Schools for Salvationist youth, Director of Music at the Army's National Singing Company Camp, guest speaker at various Divisional Music Leaders' Conferences, and conductor of the famous National Songsters. From 1963 to 1984 Muriel was Songster Leader of the prestigious Hendon Songster Brigade, touring the country and even making visits overseas. In retirement she has sustained her musical interests, applying her considerable expertise at various national events and at her own corps at Staines.

Commissioner Dinsdale Pender

* * *